Penguin Book 2501

The Penguin Book of Lost Worlds · 1

Leonard Cottrell, born in 1913 at Tettenhall, near Wolverhampton, is the author of twenty-five books, principally on archaeology and history and most of which have been published in the United States and Europe as well as in Britain. Among his best-known works are *The Bull of Minos*, *The Lost Pharaohs*, *The Anvil of Civilisation*, and *The Lion Gate*.

Educated at King Edward's Grammar School, Birmingham, he decided, while still at school, to become a writer. He first moved through advertising and journalism to the B.B.C. where, from 1942 to 1959, he wrote and produced many documentary programmes both for radio and television. His lifelong interest in archaeology and history eventually led him to write B.B.C. programmes and then books on these subjects. His first book on archaeology, *The Lost Pharaohs*, was published in 1949.

Leonard Cottrell regards his role as a professional writer as that of interpreter between the professional archaeologist and the informed layman, and tries to please the latter without offending the former. He resigned from the B.B.C. in 1959 in order to concentrate on writing and lives with his wife, a poet, in Sussex.

The Penguin Book of
LOST WORLDS

Leonard Cottrell

Volume One
Egypt, Mesopotamia,
and the Indus

Penguin Books Ltd, Harmondsworth, Middlesex, England
Penguin Books, Australia Ltd, Ringwood, Victoria, Australia

English-language edition of *The Horizon Book of Lost Worlds*
first published in the U.S.A. by
American Heritage Publishing Co., Inc., 1962

This shortened edition published as
The Penguin Book of Lost Worlds (two volumes)
by Penguin Books 1966

Made and printed in Great Britain by
Hazell Watson & Viney Ltd, Aylesbury, Bucks
Set in Monotype Baskerville

Design by Burns/Price

FRONTISPIECE: The Hypostyle Hall, Karnak

Contents

Names and Dates

The past leads us to places with strange names and introduces us to people whose names are even stranger. In many cases there is no general agreement, even among scholars, as to how these should be spelled. The spelling used in these pages follows what seemed to be the most common usage and the simplest forms, with every effort to maintain reasonable consistency. So too there is often disagreement among the most knowledgeable authorities in the matter of dates. The chronology of the ancient world is in a constant state of flux; dates are more frequently than not interdependent, and when one is changed in the light of new discoveries, in time – sometimes slowly and erratically through the medium of scholarly publications – scores of others are dislocated from their tentatively established positions. Here again, in the chart on pages 8 and 9 and throughout the text, a reasonable consistency in relation to the most generally accepted and qualified opinion has been aimed at, but in a great many cases, the dates that are indicated must still be considered only approximate.

TIME CHART

EGYPT		MESOPOTAMIA		CRETE AND MAINLAN
Predynastic Period				
Old Kingdom	**3100–2160**	**Jemdet Nasr Period**	**3200–3000**	
Union of Egypt	3100	Rise of Sumerian city-states	before 3000	
		Early Dynastic Period	**3000–2370**	**Rise of Cretan Civilization**
Third Dynasty	2670–2600			Neolithic settlement at Dimin
Step Pyramid	2650			
Cheops' Pyramid	2575	Royal Tombs of Ur	2500	
		Sargon	c. 2370	
Period of Anarchy	2160–2133	**Sumerian Revival**	**2230–2000**	
		Building of great Ur ziggurat	2100	
Middle Kingdom	**2133–1625**	**Old Babylonian Period**	**2000–1595**	**Mycenaeans Enter Greece**
		Age of Mari	c. 1800	
		Hammurabi	1792–1750	
Rise of Osiris cult				**Height of Cretan Culture**
				Building of great palaces
				Minoan domination of the sea
Hyksos Domination	1700–1567			Development of Linear A scrip
New Kingdom	**1567–1085**	Hittites sack Babylon	1595	Grave circles at Mycenae
Eighteenth Dynasty	1567–1320	**Middle Babylonian Period**	**after 1595**	
				Development of Linear B scrip
Empire of Tuthmosis III	1482–1450			**Mycenaeans Rule in Crete**
Akhenaten	1379–1361	Kassites rule Babylon		Destruction of palaces
Tutankhamen	1361–1352			and fall of Minoan civilization
Ramesses II	1304–1237			Mycenaean maritime suprema
Temples of Karnak				
and Abu Simbel				Trojan War
Exodus of the Hebrews	1240			Fall of Mycenaean centres
Great Invasion of Sea Peoples	1191			
		Assyrian Period	**1115–612**	**Dorian Invasion**
Late Period	**1085–525**	Conquests of Tiglath-pileser I	1115–1077	Final destruction of Mycenae
				Dark Age
Assyrians conquer Egypt	671	Height of Assyrian power	875–630	
Saite Period	664–525	Fall of Nineveh	612	Homer
		Neo-Babylonian Period	**612–538**	
		Nebuchadnezzar II	c. 600	**Classical Age of Greece**
Persian Domination	**525–404**	**Persian Rule**	**538–331**	Persians invade Greece
Herodotus visits Egypt	c. 450	Herodotus visits Babylon	c. 450	Herodotus
Alexander the Great conquers Egypt	332	Alexander conquers Babylon	331	Alexander the Great
Ptolemaic Period	**323–30**			
Cleopatra	69–30			

EECE	ANATOLIA AND THE LEVANT		OTHERS		
					3000
00–1900					
2700					
	Egypt trades with Byblos	2600			
	Troy II	2500–2250	**Indus Valley Civilization**	**2500–1500**	
	Alaja Huyuk	2400–2200			
					2000
00–1700	**Hittites Enter Anatolia**	**c. 1900**			BRONZE AGE
	Assyrian traders at Kultepe	1900			
er 1700					
c. 1750	Mursilis I	1620–1590			
00–1500					
er 1500	**Rise of Mitanni**	**c. 1500**			
er 1500	Phoenicians develop alphabet	c. 1500			
	Hittite Empire	**1460–1200**			
1400?	Suppiluliumas I	1380–1340			
00–1200	Battle of Kadesh	1300			
	Collapse of Hittites	1200			1250
1200	**Phrygian Occupation of Anatolia**	**1200–700**			
c. 1200	Invasions of Sea Peoples	c. 1200			
	Hebrews invade Canaan	c. 1200			
c. 1150					
1100	Neo-Hittite kingdoms in northern Syria	after 1100			1000
	Rise of Sidon and Tyre	**c. 1000**	**Villanovan Culture in Italy**	**1000**	IRON AGE
	Assyrians Dominate Levant	**875–630**	**Height of Etruscan Civilization**	**800–500**	
775?	Phoenicians found Carthage	814?	Founding of Rome	753	
492–479	**Persian Conquest of Anatolia and Levant**	**540–538**	Rome expels Tarquins	510	
c. 450			**Decline of Etruscans**	**400–200**	
c. 330			Gauls invade Italy	400–300	
			Rome conquers Veii	396	
					B.C.

1 The Kingdom of the Pharaohs

1 · The Flowering of Egypt

There is no landscape in the world quite like that of Egypt. Its strangeness, its uniqueness, have intrigued men from before the time of Herodotus, who visited Egypt almost twenty-five hundred years ago; and it continues to fascinate jet-age travellers who see more countries in a month than the 'Father of History' saw in a lifetime.

Yet the natural scene offers no spectacular variety. There are the immense margins of desert that hem in the valley of the Nile. But even in the valley there are no sky-reflecting lakes and fjords, no woods and meadows such as excite interest in other landscapes. One Egyptian village looks exactly like another, and the pattern of vegetation hardly changes from the Sudanese border in the south to the Mediterranean in the north. Nearly all the valley is cultivated; cotton, wheat, clover, beans, rice, barley, sugar cane grow in fields of monotonous flatness, varied only by the darker green of date palms, by

The Sphinx portrays the early pharaoh Chephren as a powerful lion. In later centuries, the Egyptians forgot its original significance, and worshipped it as a representation of the sun god (compare figure of Horus, page 64).

mud-brick villages, occasionally displaying the domed shrine of the local holy man, and here and there are towns with mosques and ornate nineteenth-century villas.

Thus described, Egypt sounds dull enough. But it is not. There is the astonishing contrast between the dry, powdery, desert sand and the fecund green of the valley, a demarcation so precise and uncompromising that in places one can stand with one foot on sand and the other on soil. There is also the contrast between both these elements and the age-worn, fissured cliffs of golden limestone from which the ancient Egyptians quarried their building blocks and in which they tunnelled their tombs. Third and most important there is the sudden, heart-stopping impact of man-made stone mountains reaching into the sky; of soaring columns, exceeding the girth of forest trees, crowned by capitals which gigantically reproduce the papyrus and lotus buds with which the valley proliferated in pharaonic times.

Even without the monuments of its mighty past the lure of Egypt would not disappear. The Nile itself, rolling inexorably through a thousand miles of arid desert, the only source of fertility in an almost rainless land, is wonder enough. On either bank the strip of rich green vegetation, varying in width from a few hundred yards to several miles, supports some twenty million people. Egypt, as Herodotus remarked, is truly the gift of the Nile.

However, the remote origins of Egyptian civilization are to be found not in the river valley itself, but in the deserts that flank it on east and west. There, in the limestone cliffs and in the nearby wadis, or valleys, have been found stone implements and sometimes cave-shelters containing the bones of creatures such as the hippopotamus and buffalo, gazelle and wild ass, aurochs and ostrich. For the earliest ancestors of the ancient Egyptians were not cultivators but hunters who pursued these animals over twelve thousand years ago, when Egypt still received enough rain to provide prairie-like country such as exists today in the Sudan and East Africa.

As the European glaciers receded towards the end of the last Ice Age, the climate slowly changed throughout the Near and Middle East. Over countless millenniums there was a

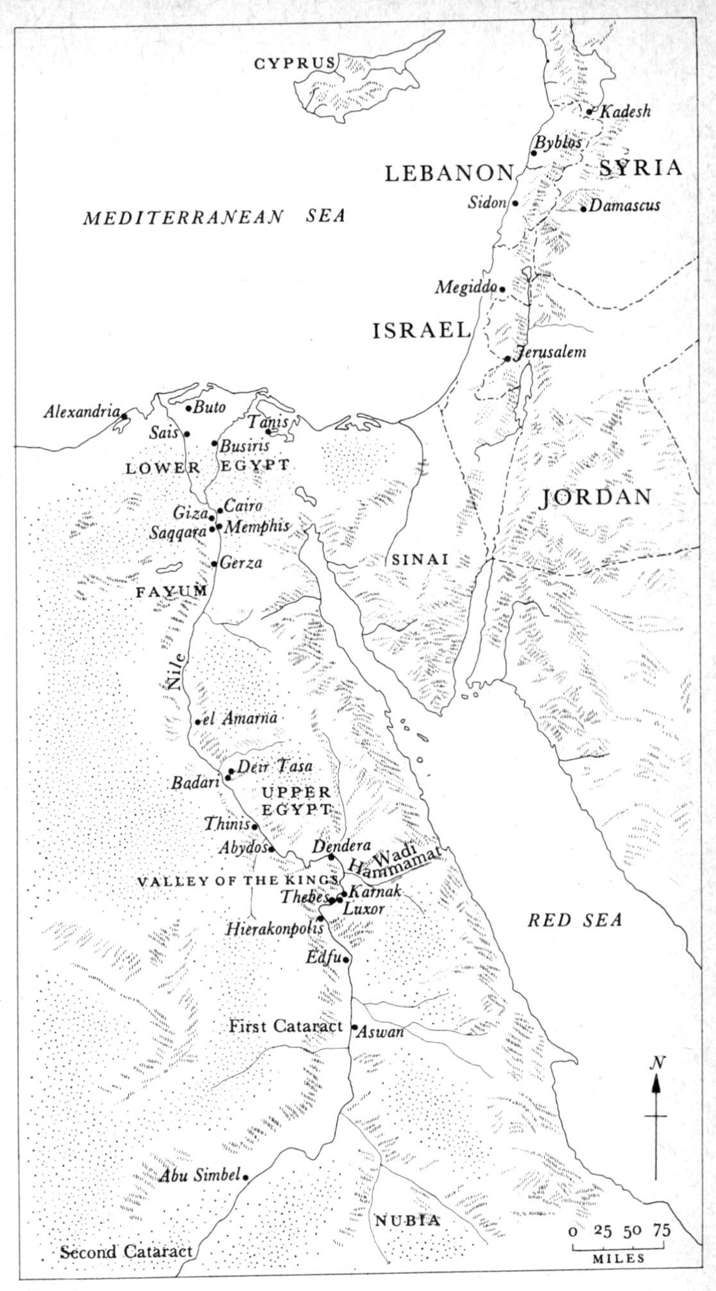
CYPRUS
Kadesh
Byblos
LEBANON
SYRIA
Sidon
Damascus
MEDITERRANEAN SEA
Megiddo
ISRAEL
Jerusalem
Alexandria
Buto
Tanis
Sais
Busiris
LOWER EGYPT
JORDAN
Cairo
Giza
Saqqara
Memphis
Gerza
SINAI
FAYUM
Nile
el Amarna
Deir Tasa
Badari
UPPER EGYPT
Thinis
Abydos
Dendera
Wadi Hammamat
VALLEY OF THE KINGS
Thebes
Karnak
Luxor
Hierakonpolis
RED SEA
Edfu
First Cataract
Aswan
N
Abu Simbel
NUBIA
0 25 50 75
MILES
Second Cataract

Egypt.

gradual drying up, and men were forced to move close to the remaining sources of the water without which they could not survive. As the Nile slowly shrank into its present bed, it left behind a series of eight terraces; and it is on the lower four of these that the worked flint tools and weapons, such as hand axes and spearheads, and the bones of slaughtered animals have been discovered. In some regions this progressive desiccation killed the rivers. But even after the rain failed in Egypt and the tributary streams which once fed it vanished, leaving only dried-up wadis to mark their former courses, still the Nile survived.

Far to the south there are in fact two Niles, the White and the Blue. The former, the main stream, rises in the great lakes Victoria and Albert in equatorial Africa. The Blue Nile, with its tributary the Atbara, flows down from the Abyssinian plateau. For a while these mountain rivers, swollen by spring rains and melted snows, and carrying a heavy burden of fertile silt, hold back the waters of the White Nile where they meet south of Khartum. Then, as their flood subsides, the White Nile is released. Thus it is those gigantic reservoirs, the lakes of central Africa, that provide the impetus that drives the waters of the Nile through a thousand miles of desert during the dry season; it is the soil scoured from the far-off highlands of Abyssinia, borne on the summer torrents of the Blue Nile and the Atbara, that provides the land with its miraculous fertility. And it is this combination of geographical circumstances that endowed Egypt with its unique heritage.

The mere existence of a large river providing a perpetual water supply and easy transport would not in itself have ensured the development of civilization. As the prairies turned to desert, animals as well as men would tend to move nearer the river valley, so that hunting would be even easier. There would be no need for men to change their nomadic life for one of permanent settlement.

For millennium after millennium the rich bounty of the Nile was ignored, while the valley dwellers continued to hunt for their food, as their ancestors had done, unaware of the potential wealth which lay beneath the marshy pools where they fished and snared wildfowl. We are dealing with a period thousands of years before the invention of written records, and no one knows who first thought of planting the seeds of wild grasses in the fertile mud and reaping the crop. Possibly the notion was brought to Egypt by immigrants from Palestine and Syria, who in turn had learned the techniques of primitive agriculture from other inhabitants of western Asia. Or, equally conceivable, the early Africans who dwelt along the Nile may have developed these elementary procedures independently.

Precise dating is impossible, but from an examination of relics found at various points along the valley, it can be established that about 5000 B.C. there were people living in Egypt who had reached a neolithic stage of development; that is to say they were using finely worked stone tools and lived mainly by hunting, which they had begun to combine with agriculture and stock raising. They buried their dead in shallow pit graves in the sand; the corpses were laid on their sides in a crouching, embryonic position, as if awaiting a second birth, and were accompanied by a few pots containing food offerings, suggesting a belief in an afterlife. Their dwellings were probably mere shelters of reeds, or mud huts.

It would be easy to dismiss the prehistoric period of Egypt, about which so tantalizingly little is known, in a few lines and to proceed quickly to the epoch of high civilization that is so much better understood. But these early centuries of effort, adaptation, and change provide the background of Egyptian culture and it is worth while to consider what may have happened.

Egypt falls naturally in two divisions, Upper (southern) and Lower (northern), with the dividing point where the narrow Nile Valley broadens out into the Delta. The character of the two regions is strongly contrasted. Upper Egypt comprises the long, tortuous river valley, coiling like a green snake between desert cliffs from the First Cataract down to Cairo; from there on Lower Egypt, like a huge fan, extends north, east, and west in a broad plain, through which the Nile branches out and continues on to the Mediterranean.

Archaeologists have long disputed in which area Egyptian civilization first struck its roots. Some have suggested that it was in the Delta, arguing that such a richly fertile area would be bound to attract settlers from an early period, once the possibilities of agriculture were understood. Another point in the Delta's favour was its nearness to the sea, to Palestine, Syria, and the Sinai Peninsula, through which influences might filter from the early Mesopotamian civilizations. Against this theory others argue with equal force that it would have been easier to colonize the southern valley of the Nile. The truth of the matter remains obscure. It might be observed in passing, however, that throughout historical times the great movements of conquest and consolidation of the 'Two Lands' came from the South.

All we know for certain is that between 5000 and 4000 B.C., perhaps even earlier, the descendants of the folk who had lived on the fringes of the Nile Valley began to move down into it. At that time the river, bordered by reeds and swamps, was still prolific in game; crocodiles and hippopotamuses basked with snouts just above the muddy water; wildfowl rose in clouds from the forest of papyrus reeds where the light skiffs of the hunters darted; harpoons and throwing sticks flashed in the sunlight; nets were lowered from frail boats of papyrus to bring up rich catches. This abundance of game persisted into historic times, and was remembered in tomb paintings and reliefs picturing life along the river in later centuries.

The primitive Egyptian lived perpetually among animals; he studied their habits in order to trap and kill them for food, and to protect himself from predators. But he also revered them, because they possessed powers superior to his own. So in time, the flying falcon became one of the insignia of royalty; the crocodile, lion, and hippopotamus were hybridized into the infernal monster that devours guilty souls; the lion, given a regal human head, became the sphinx, symbolizing kingly majesty; and the ibis with its thoughtful, knowing appearance became Thoth, the god of wisdom (and of writing).

The groups of people who early settled along the great length of the Nile Valley developed at different paces and in different ways. Scholars have given their separate, roughly consecutive cultures various impressive-sounding names, such as Tasian, Badarian, Amratian, Merimdian; but these are merely labels of convenience, derived from the modern Arabic

Fish formed a major part of the Egyptian diet, although kings were forbidden to eat any.

names of the sites where evidence of these phases was first found. Although such cultures differed markedly from one another, we should not view them as separate civilizations. From stage to stage these developments reveal a significant over-all continuity and a progressive evolution.

The funerary deposits of the fifth millennium B.C. and the early part of the fourth show that these peoples, who still lived mainly by hunting and fishing, learned to depend more heavily upon primitive agriculture and stock breeding. They grew barley and wheat, which were stored in mat-lined pits. They made clothes of animal skins, using bone needles, and already the Egyptian love of personal adornment shows itself in the form of bracelets of shell and ivory, beads of pierced stone, ivory and bone combs, and other jewellery. They also made green eye-paint by grinding malachite on slate palettes which were often carved in the shape of animals, birds, or fish. Their tools and weapons continued to be made of flint, though a few copper objects came into use in Badarian times. They used arrows tipped with flint or bone, and a certain type of mace with a pear-shaped head is often found in Amratian graves. Without benefit of the potter's wheel they fashioned earthenware vessels of excellent workmanship; and they also made vases hollowed out of stone, which was plentiful in the cliffs bordering the Nile and in the adjoining deserts. This early acquaintance with stone-working was to have tremendous consequences in later times.

Just how long this so-called Predynastic Period lasted can only be surmised. However, it culminated in one of those startling leaps forward which mankind is capable of making from time to time. Before the middle of the fourth millennium the social organization of the Egyptians seems hardly to have advanced beyond that of the primitive Dinka and Shilluk tribes who today inhabit the farther reaches of the upper Nile in the Sudan. Three hundred years later (about 3200 B.C.) the entire valley, stretching seven hundred and fifty miles from the First Cataract to the Mediterranean, was an integrated state and most of the lineaments of Egyptian civilization were already apparent. These early people had achieved a written language of a very complex nature, they could fashion beautiful objects of the hardest stone, they had undertaken a monumental architecture, their craftsmanship in copper, wood, and ivory was irreproachable. Five centuries later their descendants were raising gigantic pyramids, nearly five hundred feet high, meticulously planned and of exquisite workmanship.

Something happened that in a remarkably short time transformed this conglomeration of semi-arabic Nilotic tribesmen into a highly civilized state that lasted for almost three thousand years. What that something was we can only guess, but the archaeological evidence gives us several clues, and it is hoped that future discoveries will fill the gaps in the story. Several facts are certain. The Badarian, Amratian, Merimdian, and other neolithic cultures left nothing to compare with the mighty structures of historic times. Flinders Petrie, who made some of the greatest discoveries in Egyptian archaeology, refused at first to believe that these primitive hunter-farmers could have had any direct connexion with the builders of the great pyramids. He sought a clue in the appearance, about 3600 B.C., of a new culture, the so-called Gerzean, evidences of which have been found at Gerza and other sites in Lower Egypt, and which gradually replaced the earlier Amratian cultures at certain Upper Egyptian sites. Petrie called them the New Race and suggested that they belonged to some desert tribe whom the 'true' Egyptians permitted to live on the fringe of their territory when they themselves had become civilized. But he changed his mind when discoveries elsewhere in Egypt revealed a continuous chain of cultural development connecting all these early peoples with the Egyptians of historical times.

There have been suggestions by other Egyptologists that the impetus to civilization came from an influx of peoples, probably from the East. The inhabitants of Upper Egypt were generally long-headed and of small stature, and occasionally their skulls show signs of Negroid admixture. But in the north, archaeologists discovered the bodies of a fairly tall people with a different skull formation. Even so, the fact that they are confined mainly to the north, and not in impressively large numbers, rules out any suggestion of a complete foreign infiltration of the Nile Valley. Egypt's culture remained predominantly indigenous, although it may have been fertilized by influences from outside. Oriental influences, or interrelationships, in any case, are clearly evident.

On Gerzean pottery and later in scenes painted on mud-covered walls appear lively pictures of boats of considerable size. Since no timber suitable for such vessels was to be found in Egypt (particularly for tall masts) there must have been contact with the nearest timber-producing country – Lebanon, famous for its cedars. Indeed we can be certain of this, for such wood has been found lining tombs of the Predynastic Period. Eastern influence is again obvious, among other instances, in a knife found at Gebel el Araq, on whose ivory handle appear carved representations of ships with vertical prows and sterns and with standards, each crowned with a crescent-shaped symbol, which was a typical feature of Mesopotamian vessels.

Flint knife discovered at Gebel 'el Araq. The warriors upon it are engaged in a river battle, and the bodies of their victims can be seen floating among the ships.

On the reverse side of the handle a bearded figure is depicted standing between two rampant lions, a motif that frequently appears in early Mesopotamian seals.

Writing was developed slightly earlier in Mesopotamia than in Egypt, and some scholars believe that the idea of writing may have passed from the former land to the Nile Valley. From its earliest stages, however, the Egyptian writing system used its own distinctive signs and advanced along its own native lines. This new 'tool' had an enormously important influence on the early development of civilization in the Nile Valley.

A number of other features of predynastic Egypt clearly reveal Mesopotamian influence. One of the most striking is a type of mud-brick building with a panelled façade. Such architecture was known slightly earlier in ancient Sumer, a land where stone was almost unobtainable, and where brick construction continued to be used even in the most monumental forms. Remains of some of these early Egyptian structures may still be seen in the region of Memphis as well as in cemeteries in the south. This method of building soon developed into a characteristic Egyptian practice that was continued into historical times, and its stylistic features were copied in the great stone monuments of the early dynastic pharaohs of the succeeding centuries.

Meanwhile other techniques were introduced into Egypt. The valley dwellers still made tools and weapons of exquisitely worked flint and continued to do so until well into historical times. But they were also learning to fashion knives, axes, and spearheads of copper; they may have learned the mystery of metalworking from smiths who brought the craft from the east.

In spite of these innovations, however, the basic pattern of culture remained the same. They still worshipped the animal gods of their forefathers. Although they now had learned to live in one place, to grow crops in the Nile mud, and to store grain, their young men still stalked the wild beasts in the wadis as their ancestors had done. They lived in tribal areas scattered along the banks of the river, occasionally waging war on their neighbours or, from time to time, joining with them in a temporary alliance against a powerful enemy. At an early date each separate group adopted a certain cult sign, very roughly corresponding to a national emblem of today. Each of these provinces, or *nomes* as the Greeks later termed them, had its guardian deity, usually but not always in the form of an animal. Some of these survived throughout the entire history of ancient Egypt, such as the falcon god Horus of Hierakonpolis in Upper Egypt and the cobra goddess Wadjet of Buto in Lower Egypt.

It was a small and circumscribed world. If a man lived in the Delta, he worshipped Wadjet, knew the wide-spreading marshes of the Delta and the 'Great Green Sea' beyond. If he was a southerner, hemmed in his narrow valley, he knew the First Cataract and the water sliding over the black rocks, and must have seen the dark men who lived still farther south, and who brought the gleaming white ivory from which the craftsmen made their carved knife hilts. And his temple was that of the 'White One' of Nekheb.

Before 3200 B.C., powerful chieftains had arisen who made war on each other and celebrated their conquests on carved palettes of schist – elaborate, greatly enlarged versions of the simple slate palettes buried in the little pit graves of earlier centuries. The discovery of these commemorative palettes, together with decoratively carved knife handles and fine stone vessels, provided unmistakable links between the primitive valley dwellers and the sophisticated Egyptians who lived under the rule of the great pharaohs.

One palette shows a group of roughly square shapes with serrated edges, each containing a number of crude symbols in which are plant and animal forms. Standing on top of the squares are various animals – including a lion, a scorpion, and a falcon – apparently attacking the squares with picks. Egyptologists have interpreted this design as follows. Each of the squares represents a fortified city (the serrations are the projecting towers or bastions of a city wall). The plant or animal figures inside are the cult signs or emblems of the cities; the triumphant figures above with their picks represent the successful attackers of the stricken towns. Similar indications of the turbulence that preceded the unification of Egypt can be seen in warring figures on the Gebel el Araq knife handle, where combatants attack one another with clubs and sticks.

The palette of Narmer.

The most dramatic of all these discoveries was made in 1898 in the temple at Hierakonpolis in Upper Egypt. There was unearthed a magnificent example of the large palettes, in perfect condition, one of the most important historical documents ever found in Egypt. Dominating the scene on one side is a figure wearing the Egyptian kilt that is so familiar from innumerable later representations; on his head is the tall crown of Upper Egypt and his right hand grasps a mace, while his left is entwined in the hair of a kneeling bearded figure obviously representing an enemy. On the other side of the palette the same dominant figure wears the crown of Lower Egypt, and on each side, at the top in a central position, is a hieroglyphic inscription that reads 'Narmer'. Each of these inscriptions

Detail from the reverse of the palette of Narmer.

is contained within a *serekh*, a symbolic design representing the panelled façade of the royal palace.

The significance of this discovery was tremendous, because here, for the first time, archaeological evidence could be linked with written records. For according to the later historian Manetho, Upper and Lower Egypt were unified by a conqueror from the south who first brought the entire country under one rule about 3200 B.C. His name, in Greek, was Menes, whom scholars have identified with the first Egyptian pharaoh, Narmer.

Manetho lived in the third century B.C. when Egypt was ruled by the Ptolemies. He compiled a list of Egyptian kings from the earliest known pharaohs, dividing it into thirty-one dynasties, each representing the period during which successive generations of one family ruled the land. The list has survived only in copies which are manifestly inadequate and in part inaccurate, but for lack of a better, Egyptologists continue to use this framework, modifying it from time to time in the light of new archaeological and philological research. Until the last decade of the past century no trace of the twenty-six pharaohs listed by Manetho as having ruled during the first three dynasties, a period that he claimed covered several centuries, had been unearthed. In the 1894 edition of his history of Egypt, Petrie unequivocally stated that the chronicle of those early dynasties could only be regarded as 'a series of statements made by a state chronographer, about three thousand years after that date, concerning a period of which he had no contemporary material'. Yet the Fourth Dynasty was magnificently represented by the Great Pyramid of Cheops and all it implied concerning the development of technology and civilization. What had happened that could explain this almost miraculous flowering? Could this gap ever be filled?

The answers came in a series of dramatic discoveries, all made within a decade. Narmer's palette proved beyond doubt that the first king of the First Dynasty was no myth. Two years earlier a French scholar, É. Amélineau, had made an even more sensational discovery near Abydos, in Upper Egypt. West of the well-known temple of Sethi I, a mile beyond the cultivated area, rose a desert mound called by the Arabs Umm el Gaab, Mother of Pots. It was littered with potsherds, fragments of votive offerings brought there by ancient Egyptian worshippers who believed it to be the burial place of Osiris, the god of death and resurrection. Ruthlessly searching for saleable antiquities, and thus doing considerable damage to the remains, Amélineau came upon a large number of mud-brick tombs or *mastabas* (an Arabic word for the rectangular mud benches which still may be seen outside Arab houses and which such tombs resemble). These structures were already in a disastrous state of ruin before Amélineau got at them; but on jar sealings, bits of inscribed ivory, and other fragmentary relics there were the names of a number of early Egyptian kings.

A little later Petrie made a much more thorough and scientific excavation of the site. After months of patient effort he was able to plan the layout of each tomb, and to recover a considerable number of the inscribed stone vessels, jar sealings, ivory and ebony tablets; he also found several large carved stelae. Meanwhile other scholars had applied themselves to the study of the royal names discovered by Amélineau. It was a dramatic moment, and a landmark in the history of Egyptology, when it was announced that here undoubtedly were tangible records of some of Manetho's kings of the First and Second Dynasties, monarchs who had ruled Egypt at the dawn of her dynastic history.

At first the mastabas found at Abydos were regarded as the tombs of these early pharaohs, which had been rifled in antiquity so that not a fragment of their bodies remained. Since then, however, fourteen large, impressive mastabas of the First Dynasty have been excavated at Saqqara, near ancient Memphis, at the junction of Upper and Lower Egypt. We are told by Manetho that after his conquest of the country Narmer moved his capital to this point, so it has been argued that the real tombs were at Saqqara, and that those at Abydos were cenotaphs, probably built there because the First and Second Dynasty kings came from the town of Thinis near by; Manetho called them the 'Thinite Kings'. The matter is still being warmly discussed, and the final answer may be slow in coming.

However, as a consequence of all this, whereas the 1894 edition of Petrie's history covered the whole of predynastic Egyptian history in eight pages, that of 1902 contained concrete historical information concerning most of the kings who ruled before Snofru, first king of the Fourth Dynasty, with an account of their tombs, inscriptions, furniture, and art.

The discoveries by Petrie and V. E. Quibbell of the predynastic cemeteries at Naqada and Ballas helped to complete the story, and from a careful examination of the contents of these tombs and the Abydos mastabas, it was possible to trace a continuous development from the primitive hunter-farmers who moved down from the desert into the Nile Valley, some seven thousand years ago, to the later Egyptians whose colossal monuments can still awe us in the twentieth century.

We might pause to reconsider why one of the earliest and longest-lived civilizations in the world should have burgeoned in Egypt. We surmize that it was the result of a geographical accident and of the political unity that was at first imposed by force (and thereafter maintained by intelligent, far-seeing rulers) on a population that might have continued at a primitive level of culture for a long period of time. One essential to the creation of civilization is easy communication, which in Egypt was provided by the Nile. A second is fertile soil, in this case ensured by the annual flooding of the river. A third vital element is some directing intelligence. Since early Egyptian historical records are as scanty and incomplete as they are, we cannot know what kind of men ruled the country during the first three dynasties; but among them, surely, there must have been men of genius. Only men of high intellectual calibre and forceful character could have transformed a congeries of independent tribes, each with its own insular traditions, into a homogeneous state. Narmer may have been such a man.

When he put an end to centuries of inter-tribal strife and brought the entire country under his rule, Narmer became the master of a land that required only the organized effort of its inhabitants to realize its ample resources. The Egyptian year was divided into three seasons beginning with the rise of the Nile, the 'inundation', followed by the 'emergence of the fields from the waters' (cultivation), and then the 'deficiency of water', the drought (harvest). From early times the swollen river spread out across the valley, drowning the fields and leaving only occasional reedy mudbanks showing above a waste of brown water. When the waters went down they left behind the mud, and then came the time of sowing. Deep ploughing and fertilizing were not necessary. All that was required was to hoe or plough shallow channels in the rich silt, plant crops, and wait for them to ripen. But if Egypt was the 'gift of the Nile', sometimes that gift was withheld. There would be a 'bad Nile' when the flood was unusually low; then famine would follow. Or at other times the great river roared down the valley in an uncontrollable torrent, sweeping away men and beasts along with the frail mud-brick buildings in its path. The Nile could bring life or death, prosperity or disaster. It was to this vital problem that the Egyptian intellectual class, its priest-technicians, applied their minds.

Over the centuries the Egyptians learned how to control the flood waters, to conserve and channel them during the long dry season, and to preserve the precious top soil with a complex system of canals, dikes, and catchments. Such a system of irrigation could only be accomplished by large bodies of people working together, and this called for organization and discipline. The development of this intelligently directed communal effort marked an important step in the advance of Egyptian civilization. The necessity of re-defining land boundaries after floods had washed them away led to the development of an accurate system of surveying; the necessity of keeping records of crop yield encouraged the Egyptians to develop their writing system without which, in turn, the administration of the state would not have been possible.

The Third Dynasty started about 2670 B.C., and ushered in what is known as the Old Kingdom, Egypt's first golden age. The era lasted through the Sixth Dynasty, or for about five hundred years. The pharaohs of this epoch enjoyed a concentration of power which, once lost, was never fully recovered. Their sculptured portraits reflect this majesty and are among the highest achievements of Egyptian art. It was during this period that Egyptian architecture developed its most familiar and lasting forms, the great pyramids, those almost incredible masses of masonry whose construction demanded such an enormous expenditure of wealth, labour, and skilled direction.

Manetho tersely notes that it was one Imhotep who first taught the Egyptians to build in stone, and the ancient chronicler adds, 'he also improved the writing'. This is all he has to

tell us about the architect who lived some twenty-three hundred or more years earlier – a man who must have been one of the great geniuses of Egypt. Imhotep was the vizier (or prime minister) of Djoser, second pharaoh of the Third Dynasty. The Greeks knew him, at least by reputation, under the name Imouthes, and identified him with their god of medicine, Aesculapius. At the time when Greek traders settled in Egypt, scribes poured out a libation to him before beginning their work. His name and his titles appear on the base of a statue of Djoser found at Saqqara. Such an honour was rare when all great works were routinely ascribed to the pharaoh; so we are justified in assuming that it was Imhotep, not Djoser, who was responsible for raising the first great stone building on earth, the Step Pyramid at Saqqara. It is the oldest, most awe-inspiring, monumental stone structure in the world.

The Step Pyramid was begun as a large stone mastaba; later Imhotep enlarged it in stages, superimposing a number

Taxes were usually paid in kind with hides, labour, or agricultural produce. Having failed to fulfil their tax assessment, the overseers at left kneel before an official for judgement. While seated scribes record their cases, one delinquent villager is punished with a whipping.

Columns of King Djoser's funerary temple adjoining the Step Pyramid at Saqqara.

of progressively smaller mastabas on top of one another. But here we are looking not only at a royal tomb. Djoser's 'House of Eternity' was surrounded by various dummy buildings and courts that almost certainly reproduced the mud-brick palace and temples and the enclosures that once served the pharaoh in his earthly capital at Memphis. The entire complex, which has been partly restored, was once enclosed by a thirty-four-foot wall of panelled design whose perimeter extended for more than a mile.

One enters the pyramid on its north side, descends a long, sloping corridor, and eventually looks down into a pit ninety feet deep. At the bottom lies the granite burial chamber with a hole in the top to admit the royal body, sealed by a granite plug weighing several tons. About this chamber are rooms cut out of the solid rock, one hundred feet beneath the surface of the desert, one of them still lined with green-blue glazed tile panels imitating reed mats which may once have adorned the rooms of Djoser's palace. Similarly, the engaged, fluted columns of the entrance colonnade are reproductions in stone of the bundled reeds that supported the roof of public and domestic buildings; the ponderous stone doors, perpetually ajar, reproduce down to the last detail the wooden doors of early palace architecture.

Djoser's pyramid was built of small stone blocks, little bigger than the mud bricks that were their prototypes. But within less than a century such uneconomic building methods were abandoned. Instead, accurately cut blocks of white limestone weighing several tons each were used. Some of the larger granite monoliths used for burial chambers weighed as much as fifty tons. The Great Pyramid built for Pharaoh Cheops shortly after 2600 B.C. incorporated more than two million

The pyramid of Cheops [right] and that of his son Chephren.

stone blocks averaging two-and-a-half tons in weight in the main structure, which was over seven hundred and fifty feet along each base line and rose to a height of nearly five hundred feet. (When he laid eyes on this stupendous monument, Napoleon estimated that it contained enough building material to make a wall ten feet high around most of France.) The structure is oriented to within one-twentieth of a degree to the true north. The stone blocks were cut with such precision that the blade of a knife could not be inserted between them when they were laid in place. Moreover, the giant granite elements had been quarried in far-off Aswan and brought by boat or raft along the six-hundred-mile length of the river. And the entire building was originally sheathed in a skin of smoothly finished white limestone. All this was achieved almost five thousand years ago by a people whose only mechanical devices were the lever, the roller, and the inclined plane. They did not even know the wheel or the block and tackle – they had only simple tools.

When Djoser was put to rest beneath his Step Pyramid so long ago, recorded Egyptian history had barely begun; over twenty-six hundred years were to pass before the last pharaoh ruled the land. Yet the pattern of Egyptian civilization had already been set. The features of Egyptian culture had become fixed in a rigid mould, and it changed very little in character throughout the long course of ancient Egyptian history.

Why did this civilization assume the pattern it did? Why did they bury one frail mortal, a pharaoh though he be, so

Apart from his pyramid and a few inscriptions that commemorate mining expeditions, relics of Cheops' reign are few. Among them is this tiny ivory statue of him.

richly bedizened, under millions of tons of precisely cut stone? What conviction could have persuaded them to expend untold man-hours in raising innumerable tombs, richer than the houses their owners occupied in life, adorned with elaborate and beautifully executed sculpture and painting which no human being was intended to see? Why did they worship and make sacrifices to fantastic gods with human bodies and animal heads?

The answer is not easy to give. The theological system of the Egyptians remains somewhat puzzling to us, as indeed it probably was to most Egyptians. They inherited what seems to us a hodge-podge of widely varying customs and beliefs, many of them mutually inconsistent, and stemming back to those far-distant times when their ancestors lived in tribal communities along the Nile Valley, each with its local deity. As one scholar has written:

> The impression made on the modern mind is that of a people searching in the dark for a key to truth and, having found not one but many keys resembling the pattern of the lock, retaining all lest perchance the appropriate one should be discarded.

The two principal religious cults which helped to shape Egypt's culture throughout her long history were those of Re, the sun god, and Osiris, god of death and resurrection. They originated independently, and there was never any logical connexion between them, except that both can be taken to symbolize birth, death, and renewal. The sun is an omnipresent force in Egypt. Every day, in that hot, cloudless sky, the fiery disk is seen rising behind the eastern hills, arching across the valley, and descending below the rim of the western desert. It is easy to see why the Egyptians adored the sun as the giver of life and saw in its progress the pattern of life perpetually renewed. Every night Re died in the west and every morning he was reborn in the east. It was doubtless for this reason that the Egyptians buried their dead in the west; indeed one of the names for the dead was the 'Westerners'. The centre of the Re cult was at Heliopolis not far from the city of Memphis which Narmer made his capital after the unification of Egypt. This would help to account for the predominance of the sun god from the early dynastic period to the end of the Old Kingdom.

The cult of Osiris, his wife and sister Isis, and their son Horus involves a myth that according to one version may be summarized as follows. In the beginning there was only a waste of waters, the primeval ocean on which appeared an egg from which was born Re, the sun god. He had four children, Geb, the earth god, Shu and Tefnut, gods of the atmosphere, and Nut, the sky goddess. Shu and Tefnut, planting their feet on Geb, raised Nut to the heavens. In some later Egyptian tombs a painting on the ceiling, or under the lid of the sarco-

A papyrus discovered in the tomb of a priest. It shows the god of the air, Shu, separating the earth from the sky, while ram-headed deities assist him. Above Shu's head is the sky goddess, Nut, her body covered with stars, and the hieroglyphic sign for west written in front of her face. A bird, representing the soul of the priest for whom the papyrus was made, is shown riding along the circuit of the sun in a small boat. The sky goddess touches the level of the earth only with her fingers and toes. Far beneath her, her husband, Geb, the earth god, lies exhausted after struggling against Shu's efforts to separate him from the sky. His bent knees and elbows represent the mountains and valleys on the surface of the earth.

phagus, represents Nut as a woman whose body is arched across the sky.

This is certainly a primitive creation myth with which the cult of Osiris was later integrated. Osiris was the son of Geb and Nut, who had three other children, Isis, Nephthys, and Seth. Osiris married his sister Isis (within the Egyptian royal family brother-sister marriages became common practice), and subsequently succeeded to the throne of Egypt, which he governed wisely and humanely. He persuaded the Egyptians to give up cannibalism, and introduced them to useful arts and crafts. (Surely the prototype of Osiris was an earthly ruler who

was later deified or became identified with an already existing god.) His wicked brother Seth was jealous and plotted against him. Eventually Seth succeeded in killing Osiris by treachery, later dissecting the body and burying the pieces in various parts of Egypt, all except the penis that he threw into the river at Oxyrhyncus. The head was buried at Abydos, later an important cult centre to which pilgrimages were made.

Isis, the faithful wife, recovered the parts of her husband's body (all save the organ of generation) and, with the help of the god Anubis, reassembled and reanimated the corpse. But since Osiris had now lost his reproductive powers he could no longer rule over the living. He therefore became god of the dead and judge of souls.

That was the first part of the myth. The resurrection of Osiris bears resemblances to myths underlying the fertility cults practised by other peoples. The second part concerns Horus, the devoted and loyal son of Osiris, who sought out Seth and eventually slew him, though in the fight Seth plucked out his nephew's eye, which was later restored to him by the god Thoth. (The 'eye of Horus' figures prominently in many Egyptian religious monuments and inscriptions as a symbol of sacrifice.) Thus, after avenging his father, Horus himself ascended the throne of Egypt.

That the Osiris-Isis-Horus myth took such a hold on the Egyptians' imagination, that it survived for more than thirty centuries was due, surely, to its humanity. The cult of the sun god and his sacred bark into which only the king could enter was an austere conception, the product of an intellectual priestly class. But every wife could identify herself with the faithful Isis, every son with Horus, every father with Osiris. As for the second part of the story, the revenge of Horus, it may be significant that Europe's greatest psychological drama closely parallels this ancient myth. Claudius treacherously kills his royal brother to gain the throne; Hamlet, his nephew, kills Claudius to avenge his father.

It is important to outline these myths, for from an early date Pharaoh was considered both god and king. He proclaimed himself Horus, who became Osiris on death. Later he became the divine son of the sun god Re. This title, which probably originated when the pharaohs ruled from Memphis, near the Heliopolitan centre of the sun cult, was retained down to the last dynasty, even when, with the rise of the Theban kings, the Theban god Amen had come to be associated with the sun god as Amen-Re.

In very early times the king may have been sacrificed after a

The funerary deity, Anubis, is shown with a jackal head. Next to him are Re, the sun god, and Osiris, the king of the dead, who is seated upon the throne of Egypt.

certain number of years to propitiate the gods and to renew the fertility of the soil. This sacrificial role was not forgotten in later times. Among the reliefs that have survived in the Step Pyramid complex we see Djoser in a running posture, wearing the crowns of Upper and Lower Egypt, but otherwise almost naked. And in the great courtyard to the south of his pyramid, archaeologists have discovered the remains of two posts, like those of a race-course. It has been suggested that the reliefs depict part of the *heb-sed*, a festival in which the monarch had to prove his vitality by sprinting around a set course. Once he

Djoser running.

would have been killed when his powers started to wane, but in these later times his strength could be magically renewed by a ritualistic formula that represented him passing this test of vigour.

This tenacity of ancient religious beliefs is further disclosed by inscriptions on the walls of pyramid chambers of the Fifth and Sixth Dynasties. These so-called Pyramid Texts, a large body of magic formulas that ensured the happiness and fulfilment of Pharaoh in the next world, include a description of the dead king sallying forth to lasso and kill the gods for his cooking pot. This cannibalistic spell is obviously a relic of that far-off time when the ancestors of the pyramid builders were ruled by a king who feasted ritually on the bodies of his foes in order to bring the rain – a custom that has been practised by barbarous tribes until fairly recent days.

Throughout historic times it was the function of the king to perform the necessary sacrifices to the principal gods. In this way he protected his subjects by acting as intermediary between them and the unseen, unknown powers that governed men's lives. The prosperity of the land, the fertility of the soil, and the survival of his people depended ultimately upon the king. In their eyes he was divinity incarnate, and after his earthly death he would continue to watch over Egypt's welfare as he had done in life.

Unless we accept the fact that these and other religious beliefs were valid to the Egyptians, the pyramids, rock-cut tombs, gigantic temples, and all the rest of their funerary art will appear only as curiosities, perversions of the human mind. But they were in fact practical devices that grew out of the conditions of human life as the Egyptians lived it and as they understood the meaning of existence. They provide insights into customs and beliefs that have long since vanished.

It is difficult to penetrate the minds of people who lived at a time so remote from our own. Certainly the ancient Egyptians believed in what we call the soul. In fact they recognized two souls, the *ba* and the *ka*. The former they represented in hieroglyphs by a figure of a little, bearded, human-headed bird. The hieroglyph for the *ka* consisted of two human arms bent at the elbow, to which was sometimes added a bearded human figure wearing them as a crown. Neither of these entities could survive into afterlife unless the body of the deceased was preserved and protected from violation, and it was for this reason that the Egyptians practised mummification.

In predynastic times when the dead were buried in shallow pits, the dry sand preserved them to such an astonishing degree that even today there are corpses, interred without embalming, which still retain their skin and hair. Such graves could be robbed; once the Egyptians began to protect them by sinking shafts into the rock, and covering these with mud-brick or stone superstructures, the bodies tended to decompose unless preventive measures were taken. This led the Egyptians to develop the technique of artificial preservation at least as early as the Second Dynasty. There was nothing mysterious about the embalming process, which could probably be improved upon today. The most ancient mummy known was found by Petrie at Medum and dates from the Fifth Dynasty. Long before, however, attempts were made to make the corpse appear lifelike by wrapping each limb separately and even inserting resin-soaked pads under the wrappings to give the body the appropriate contours.

As time passed this method was refined until there grew a large corps of skilled embalmers who even had a tariff of charges; the price varied according to the complexity of the process and the work involved. The *de luxe* method, reserved for royalty and high officials, took several months. First the embalmers made an incision and removed the viscera: heart, liver, lungs, intestines – all the most decomposable parts. These were installed separately in a set of stone vessels, later called canopic jars, each consigned to the protection of a particular god. The heart, however, was re-inserted within the body, probably because the Egyptians regarded the heart and not the brain as the seat of intelligence.

Meanwhile the eviscerated corpse was allowed to soak for about seventy days in a bath of nitre, after which it was removed, dried, and wrapped in resinous strips of linen. But it was in the process preceding this that the embalmer exhibited his greatest skill. By placing linen pads under the skin he was able to fill out the sunken cheeks and give an appearance of firmness to the limbs which, before wrapping, were adorned with fine jewellery and ornaments.

This, of course, represents the ultimate in embalming technique, as practised a thousand years after the end of the Old Kingdom. The bodies of the pyramid builders may not have been so skilfully preserved, though we cannot be sure, since none have survived. However, even in the age of Cheops, the embalming process took several months, as we know from written evidence. We are told that 272 days passed between the death and burial of his grandchild Queen Meresankh III. Again, when the American archaeologist George Reisner discovered the tomb of Cheops' mother, Queen Hetepheres, though the body was missing the alabaster vessel containing her viscera was still in place and in one of the canopic compartments liquid embalming fluid was still preserved. These internal organs, together with the queen's gold throne, silver anklets, make-up box, and other equipment can still be inspected in the Cairo Museum – an intriguing juxtaposition of mortality and vanity.

As additional protection the form of the deceased was reproduced in sculptures and in paintings to provide other substitute refuges for the spirits. These likenesses, buried in the silent chambers of the dead, were not intended to be seen by human eyes. They were in effect a supplementary form of afterlife insurance. The main point was to preserve the appearance of the body so that the *ba* or *ka* would recognize it even if the mortal remains that they represented were destroyed. The dead also had to be provided with food, drink, and other material needs of a living body. In early days these were stockpiled in royal tombs in enormous quantities and later supplemented by regular offerings. Actual physical remains of these tomb offerings have been found. One such, discovered by W. B. Emery in a Second Dynasty mastaba, consisted of soup, ribs of beef, kidneys, pigeon, quail, fish, fruit, bread and cake.

Other peoples to our own day have also believed devoutly in an afterlife, but none have taken such elaborate precautions to assure life beyond death. Future generations would gain little understanding of our western way of life from our somewhat nebulous picture of heaven. 'You can't take it with you', we say. Not so the Egyptians. They believed they could, and their picture of the hereafter was of a life lived much as it had been known on earth. There was nothing morbid about their concept of death. Rather it projected the industrious, cheerful, and plentiful life that the Egyptian, with reasonable expectation, wished to enjoy everlastingly.

They attached a magical value to representations of their possessions – their families and servants as well as their houses, gardens, flocks, and herds – whereby these models, paintings, and reliefs were infested with all the attributes of the real thing, throughout eternity.

In representing the world about him the ancient Egyptian artist observed relatively fixed conventions that were accepted and understood by his contemporary audience. Human figures are scaled according to their importance in the Egyptian social and hierarchical scheme. The pharaoh or a high official is depicted much larger than the servants or commoners who attend him at the banquet table or who swarm about him in the fields and in the marshes. Perspective as we understand it was not attempted. The various elements of a scene are arranged in a series of horizontal registers, nearer objects being indicated in the lower panels, and in ascending order, the more distant ones shown above. To represent the human figure the Egyptian painter selected the most characteristic and easily recognizable aspects of his subjects and combined them in an image that never meets normal vision. The head is shown in profile but the eye within it appears in front view; the torso is also shown as seen from the front, but the arms and legs in profile. Rigid and unnatural as the conventions may seem by the traditional standards of western art, to the Egyptian they conveyed an impression of the complete and enduring power of the human body.

When the king died the chambers of his sepulchre were filled with rich furniture – beds, couches, and chairs inlaid with ivory and gold, his chests of clothing – as well as weapons, ornaments, food, and wine, to serve his every need in the hereafter. More than eighty pyramids, many of them extremely large, although only one rivalled Cheops' pyramid in size, were built to protect the mortal remains of the god-kings and their possessions. And every one of these bodies was stripped, destroyed, and robbed of its precious equipment thousands of years ago. All that survives are the empty shells of the sacred tombs. The bodies of the royal dead have disappeared, as have those of the countless hordes who laboured to build for the great ones their eternal homes.

Yet, ironically, while the personalities and achievements of the god-kings have been reduced to mere names, those of their noble servants – and of even servants of those servants – have more substance for us. From the Fourth Dynasty on it was customary for the great officials to build mastabas near Pharaoh's pyramid. Whole streets of these tombs have survived, and in some of the larger examples there are brilliant reliefs depicting the aspects of the dead man's earthly life which he particularly wished to be perpetuated in the hereafter. These often follow set patterns; there are scenes of hunting with the nobleman harpooning hippopotamuses or hurling a throwing stick at wildfowl while delicately poised in a light skiff of papyrus reeds; sometimes his wife or daughter is shown holding his leg in a companionable spirit, and a servant crouches in the bow of the boat to pick up the game. There are also feasting scenes. In these we see the great man and his wife seated on stately chairs and receiving their guests; tables are spread with delicacies, servants pour wine, and dancing girls perform to the sound of flutes, harps, and drums. The food served at such banquets can be recognized from these sculptured and painted representations. The tomb of the vizier Kagemni contains a pillared hall with adjoining rooms, one of which is adorned with reliefs showing ducks in a duckpond and fishermen coming home with their catch. More extraordinary is a scene showing hyenas being artificially fattened for the vizier's table; Egyptian taste in food did not always coincide with ours. Forced feeding of animals to fatten them was quite common and is frequently depicted. *Pâté de foie gras* has a history of at least five thousand years.

The fact that women are shown sharing these social pleaures with men distinguishes the ancient Egyptians from some other Oriental civilizations; the wife of an official is given equal prominence with her husband, and frequently the couple

Force-feeding fowl.

Mycerinus and his queen.

are shown in an affectionate posture, with her arm around his waist – as occasionally, indeed, are a pharaoh and his spouse. These ladies of so long ago have an elegance and sophistication which appeal strongly to an age in which the slim, svelte line is again fashionable. Even their make-up is not too exotic to us; they reddened their lips, painted their fingernails and toenails, and used heavy eye shadow. Writers on ancient Egypt often call attention to the fact that a set of workman's tools – say those of a carpenter – would be immediately familiar to his modern counterpart. This is true; but it is equally true that a modern western woman, faced with a set of ancient Egyptian cosmetics in their elegant alabaster jars and other beautifying paraphernalia, would know what to do with most of them.

Other tomb scenes show very clearly the sources of wealth

[Top] An application of lipstick. [Above] Girl, wearing little except jewellery, eye paint, and a lotus. [Left] Bronze mirror.

that supported this luxury. It came from the land. We see farm hands working in the fields, sowing and harvesting the grain; we see lines of fat cattle being driven to slaughter, and butchers with knives cutting up the carcasses; other men carry haunches of beef to the burial chamber, so that the *ka* would never lack sustenance, even if the descendants of the dead man or the priests appointed by them ceased to make real food offerings at the tomb. The intimate details often depicted in these scenes take us back into the immediate presence of these long-dead people. Sometimes hieroglyphic inscriptions introduce a line or two of comment or dialogue. One high-born lady at a noble banquet cries out, 'I want to drink till I'm drunk; my inside is like a straw', while a servant refills her goblet. In the mastaba of Mereruka, vizier of the first king of the Sixth Dynasty, one field worker calls to another, 'Where are you now, you loafer?' and the foreman exclaims, 'This barley is very good, fellow!'

On the walls of the tomb of Vizier Ptahhotep we see boys playing games. Some are trying their skill at the feat which small boys still attempt today, to rise from a sitting position while holding their toes. Another boy kneels on the ground,

Woman preparing beer by pressing mash through a sieve.

trying to confuse his playmates by catching their feet. They in turn attack him, amid cries of 'Look, you've kicked me!' and 'I've got you!' All this dialogue is faithfully recorded in the inscriptions, as for instance in a scene where fish are drying in the sun and a boy and an old man are making ropes for boat building. 'O strong youth, bring me ropes,' asks the old fellow; and the boy replies, 'O my father, here is the rope.'

Among the most amazing Old Kingdom reliefs are those in the mastaba of Ankhmahor, a high official under the pharaoh, Teti (Sixth Dynasty). It is often called 'The Physicians' Tomb' because one room contains representations of surgical operations, including circumcision and an operation on a man's toe.

Dancing scene from the 'Physicians' Tomb'.

While their companion saws a board in half, two carpenters work on a wooden beam with mallet and chisel.

Although such scenes have no special reference to Ankhmahor, these and other reliefs give this tomb a particular interest. In one of them a line of dancing girls is executing a concerted high kick which would do credit to any modern chorus line. The big toe of each barefoot dancer exactly touches the line dividing this scene from the one above; heads are thrown back, at exactly the same angle; each girl's hair is tied in a pigtail with a pompon at the end, and their arms are rhythmically raised, caught, almost photographically, in a 'frozen moment' of time.

These tomb paintings and reliefs are like windows through which we may peer into the Egyptian past. Humble men and women are often depicted with compassion and humour, as indeed are the domestic animals. One has the feeling that life for a workman or peasant on a nobleman's estate was no worse, or better, than it was, let us say, on a great estate in nineteenth-century England. There is no positive proof, but it is permissible to believe that, on the whole, Egypt was humanely and wisely governed.

The pharaohs were both divine rulers and temporal governors. Some of these men played an extremely active, creative role in the administration of the state; they appointed and supervised officials, instituted reforms, and initiated great public works. Some became capable, even brilliant, generals who led their armies in person.

Immediately beneath the pharaoh, at the second stage of the social pyramid, were large numbers of high officials, the 'senior civil servants' representing the upper echelons of the Egyptian administrative system. (Particularly in the Old Kingdom, this ruling group included the progeny of the pharaoh and his wife or his concubines, and other royal relatives, sometimes numbering hundreds.) Some were the *nomarchs* who governed the nomes or provinces. Many had purely honorary functions, such as the 'Fanbearer on the King's Right Hand', or supervised the palace staff including, of course, the royal harem. Others were priests whose function was more than sacerdotal; they not only performed rites of propitiation and sacrifice, but administered the gods' vast estates and temples. They also largely controlled the educational system. Not infrequently, and not surprisingly, court and priesthood were in conflict.

Beneath the great officers in descending order of rank and responsibility came other, lesser officials, all of whom would have been scribes, for literacy was the first prerequisite of office. Writing was taught in the temple schools, which might also be regarded as training colleges for the innumerable officials who administered Egypt. Being a scribe had many attractions, not the least of which was exemption from manual work. The ordinary Egyptian peasant or labourer was liable to be conscripted for large-scale public works such as digging ditches and repairing embankments after the annual inundation. But not the scribe. An Egyptian school exercise of a much later period contains the refrain, 'Be a scribe, who is freed from forced labour, and protected from all work'; that is manual work. The same document gives a vivid and probably exaggerated picture of the plight of the poor peasant who cannot pay his taxes:

The dwarf Seneb, with his wife and children, was an official in charge of a weaving workshop in Lower Egypt. Although not of royal blood himself, Seneb married a woman who was related to the king, after having worked his way up through the ranks of Pharaoh's service.

And now the scribe landeth on the embankment and will register the harvest. The porters carry sticks, and the Negroes palm-ribs. They say: 'Give corn.' 'There is none here' [says the peasant]. He is stretched out and beaten; he is bound and thrown into the canal. His wife is bound in his presence, his children are put in fetters. His neighbours leave them, they take to flight, and look after their corn. But the scribe, he directeth the work of all people. For him there are no taxes, for he payeth tribute in writing, and there are no dues for him. Prithee, know that.

Admittedly this comes from a prejudiced source, but there is little doubt that the labouring masses were sometimes treated with severity, even with cruelty. However there is little or no evidence that the ordinary Egyptian felt he suffered from social injustice; he did not question the established order of things. There were apparently no codified laws. Law was the word of Pharaoh, and as god Pharaoh was the personification of justice as the Egyptians understood it. He interpreted the inevitable, divine order of the world – and to the early Egyptians, at least, Egypt *was* the world – in terms of what was good, right, and equitable. This concept of the established 'rightness' of things, of what was good as opposed to what was bad, was broadly covered by the Egyptian word *maat*, a word that has no equivalent in our language.

Much that we know of the ancient Egyptians is derived from those of their own accounts that have survived. The beginnings of a written language can be found in the signs on predynastic commemorative palettes. By about 2500 B.C. the Egyptians had already a burgeoning literature. What had begun as a method of keeping records had developed into a subtle and flexible instrument of communication. Pictographs had long ceased to be merely symbols of things – heads of cattle, measures of land, wheat, wine, and oil. They had come to represent the sounds of the Egyptians' spoken language, with all its grammatical complexities, variations of meaning, and rhythm. There were, at this time, two methods of writing the language: the fully formed hieroglyphs which were usually carved in stone; and the flowing cursive style with abbreviated symbols which, like our modern handwriting, were easier to write, and which the Greeks later called hieratic. By extracting the pith from the papyrus reed that grew in the marshes along the Nile, gluing the reed strips together, and drying them, the ancient Egyptians produced a light, portable, and convenient writing material on which they wrote with fine brushes or rush pens. Our modern word *paper* is derived from *papyrus*, just as the word *Bible*, originally meaning *book*, reminds us of the port of Byblos in Lebanon, which later was the main port for the export of papyrus scrolls.

Many examples of scribes' writing materials have been found in Egyptian tombs, and a considerable number of inscribed papyri, though these represent only a minute fraction of the quantity that must once have existed. They include the earliest known medical textbooks; also letters, state records, school exercise books, religious texts, stories, and poems. Some of these documents date back to the Old Kingdom, and include tales of fantasy and wonder of which the Egyptians were very fond.

One of the latter concerns the pharaoh, Snofru, father of Cheops. In a fit of very deep depression the king asked his court magician, Djadjamankh, to devise some sort of entertainment that would distract his mind, dispel his mood. In a free version of a standard translation the popular story proceeds as follows:

. . . And Djadjamankh said to him: 'If your majesty would but go to the lake of the palace. Man a boat with all fair damsels from the inner apartments. Then will your heart be diverted when you watch them row to and fro.' . . . And his majesty replied: 'I will do this. . . . Bring me twenty paddles of ebony inlaid with gold . . . and twenty women with the fairest limbs, and with beauteous breasts and braided tresses, such as have not yet given birth, and moreover bring me twenty nets, and give these to the women instead of their clothes.' And it was done according to all that his majesty commanded. And they rowed to and fro, and the heart of his majesty was glad when he saw them row.

Then a leader became entangled with her braided hair, and her hair ornament of new malachite in the form of a fish-pendant fell into the water. And she became silent and stopped rowing, and the girls on her side became silent and stopped rowing. Then his majesty asked: 'Why do you not row?' . . . She said: 'My new fish-pendant has fallen into the water.' He had another brought to her and said: 'I give you this instead.' But she said: 'I like my own better.'

This is perhaps the most fascinating episode in the tale, for the mighty pharaoh obeyed her whim. He recalled his magician Djadjamankh, and explained his difficult position. Fortunately the magician was equal to the difficulties of the occasion. He performed the same miracle that Moses accomplished on the Red Sea a thousand years later. He parted the waters of the lake.

Then Djadjamankh said his say of magic, and he placed the one side of the water of the lake upon the other, and found the fish-pendant lying on a piece of pottery. And he brought it and gave it to its mistress. . . . Then he said his say of magic, and he brought the waters of the lake to their place.

Admittedly this is merely a folk tale, yet it must have been drawn to some degree from observed experience. The testimony of the Hebrews and tales of oppression under the pyramid builders repeated by dragonmen to Greek travellers in much later times cannot be accepted at face value. In spite of old legends of slave-driving autocrats, it would seem that the affairs of the royal family attracted general interest and that pharaoh, certainly Snofru, enjoyed the affection of his people. And it is also part of the record that when the Israelites came to Egypt at a time of famine, they received corn – probably at a fair price – from the hands of one of their own race who had won the confidence of the king.

One of the most remarkable documents that have survived is the so-called Edwin Smith Papyrus, a later copy of what was probably the earliest treatise on surgery. As the anatomist Warren Dawson has pointed out, this papyrus indicates that at an early date the Egyptians made serious attempts to understand the structure of the human body. They had studied the brain, observed that its hemispheres were patterned with convolutions, and understood that injury to it would affect other parts of the body; although in spite of their ample experience in dissection through embalming, they apparently did not discover that the brain was the seat of intelligence. They knew that the heart 'speaks' in other parts of the body, but they did not grasp the concept of the circulation of the blood, a concept, we might add, that was only defined a few hundred years ago.

They knew that certain injuries could be repaired and that others were hopeless. Ancient skulls have been found showing loose teeth fastened together with gold wire and, in at least one case, evidence of a successful operation to drain an abscess at the root of a molar. There were obviously specialists. We read of eye doctors, also 'those who know the secret and specialize in the body fluids', those who could prescribe for diseases of the lungs, bladder, stomach, and even for falling or greying hair; and bowel specialists, splendidly entitled Guardians of the Anus.

Among the drugs recommended by ancient Egyptian doctors there are a number that are still used by the modern medical profession, including acacia, anise, cassia, castor beans, wormwood, coriander, and saffron. Among the mineral substances are sodium bicarbonate, arsenic, and nitre (of which the very name is Egyptian), alum, and sulphur.

Despite such impressive testimony it would be unrealistic to regard this medical knowledge as being based on anything remotely resembling a scientific approach to medicine. Whatever was practical and efficacious in their methods was the result of a long process of trial and error. They owed it less to their own inquiring minds than to the experience of generations of ancestors who had tried out certain remedies in the past and discovered that some were effective and others less so. The same is true of their other achievements; in the field of mathematics, for instance, there exists a famous mathematical document called the Rhind Papyrus, which among other things deals with the problem of triangles. It is a highly practical and useful document, but it would be false to compare it to the productions of Euclid and Pythagoras over two thousand years later. The Greeks were more interested in pure knowledge than in its practical application. Not so the ancient Egyptians. Given the task of healing a wound, curing a disease, drawing a boundary, measuring the rise of the Nile or the movement of the stars, or levelling a site for a pyramid, they faced the problem and solved it to the best of their ability and then got on with the job. And that was as far as they went.

In the elaborate hierarchical society that so early developed in Egypt, every man and woman, from Pharaoh down, had a definite place and function; albeit people of drive and ability could and did rise from the ranks. All wealth was in kind; it was derived almost entirely from the land; and all land was, nominally, owned by the pharaoh. Using units of grain and copper as a measure of value, the Egyptian held markets, lent on interest, and developed an elaborate system of taxation. There was some internal trade although, at least in the early period, each nome was virtually self-sufficient and every royal or priestly estate had its own group of tradesmen, craftsmen, and field workers.

Foreign commerce was nominally the province of Pharaoh. Even in the Old Kingdom, Egypt traded with Lebanon, Asia Minor, the Aegean Islands, and with the Land of Punt (probably Somaliland) from which were imported perfumes and incense. From Nubia (directly to the south) Egyptians brought back, by trade or conquest, ivory, ebony, gold, ostrich feathers (for fans), myrrh (for incense), and such exotic beasts as giraffes and monkeys.

Protected by the natural barriers of barren wastelands and sea, Egypt had the advantage of developing and maintaining its unique culture, undisturbed by major foreign invasion, over a period of some two thousand years. In this comfortable isolation there was room and, except in bad times, food for everyone. On the whole the evidence suggests that the Egyptian way of life seemed good to all concerned. As we have seen, the basic pattern of civilization was established at an early date, and the Egyptians clung to this pattern with remarkable resourcefulness and with relatively minor changes throughout their long, remarkable history. We who tend to equate change with progress and revolution with historical evolution may be reminded that a static condition of harmony in the social body has, or has had, much to recommend it.

2 · Anarchy and Recovery

The pattern of Egyptian civilization, which had been set at such an early date, and which retained its basic character over such an immense span of time, was never completely rigid. Various forces – political, economic, religious – impinged upon the valley dwellers, bringing about changes that called for adaptations within the established system. We can see this develop during the middle years of the third millennium B.C. and culminate in the Sixth Dynasty, with which the Old Kingdom came to an end. The pyramids of this and the preceding dynasty are smaller than those of the Fourth Dynasty and less carefully constructed. They suggest a decline of the royal power; and when the absolute authority exercised by the early Memphite kings diminished, anarchy ensued, at least in some parts of the land.

> Plunderers are everywhere . . . the Nile is in flood, yet none ploweth . . . Every man saith: 'We know not what hath happened throughout the land.' . . . Plague stalketh through the land and blood is everywhere . . . Men do not sail to Byblos today. What can we do to get cedars for our mummies? Priests are buried with their produce, and princes are embalmed with their resin as far as the land of Keftiu [Crete?], and now they come no more . . . laughter hath perished and is no longer made. It is grief that walketh through the land, mingled with lamentations. . . . The land is left over to its weariness, as when one hath pulled up the flax . . . corn hath perished everywhere. People are stripped of clothing, perfume, and oil. Every one saith: 'There is no more.' . . . The storehouse is bare, and he that kept it lieth stretched out on the ground. . . . A thing hath been done, that happened not aforetime; it is come to this that the king hath been taken away by poor men [the royal sepulchre had been plundered] . . . he that was buried as a hawk lieth on a bier. What the pyramid hid will become empty.

Copper statue of Pepi I, one of the last pharaohs of the old Kingdom.

This lament, excerpted from what is called 'The Admonitions of the Prophet Ipuwer', criticizes an unnamed pharaoh of the Sixth Dynasty for allowing his country to fall into such a state of unrest and confusion. Though probably exaggerated, its tone makes clear the disorganization that was besetting Egypt at the time. There appear to have been civil uprisings, and we know that the pyramid tombs of Cheops, Chephren, and Mycerinus were rifled and their statues left to neglect and destruction. This occurs time and again in Egyptian history; we have noticed how the First Dynasty mastabas at Abydos and Saqqara had been plundered. Perhaps this was not the work of thieves, but the acts of contending and usurping forces within the kingdom.

How did it happen that the mighty pharaohs lost their accustomed supreme control over the land? What accounts for the disturbances that moved Ipuwer to his long and bitter lament? The kings of the later dynasties of the Old Kingdom probably overreached themselves by endeavouring to extend their power beyond its permissible limits. They could have been forced to do this by external circumstances. It was necessary to exercise some kind of control over the southern frontier, partly for purposes of security and partly for purposes of trade. Carved inscriptions on the rocky cliffs overlooking the Nile beyond the First Cataract bear the names of First and Second Dynasty kings, proving that even in that remote age royal expeditions were sent to the area. Similarly, in the north-east, in the Sinai peninsula where the Egyptians mined copper and malachite, there are rock-cut figures of the pharaohs who sent expeditions there; even as early a king as Sekhemkhet, successor to Djoser, is represented. The desert Bedouins who threatened these expeditions had to be held back; and in the west as well the warlike Libyans of the Western Desert were ever a thorn in Egypt's side.

On the southern frontier of Egypt, which was governed by powerful border lords, conditions were especially turbulent. Besides keeping watch on the Nubians to the south, these great officials conducted lucrative trading ventures across the Arabian Desert and beyond the sea to the mysterious Land of Punt, where the Egyptians obtained their supplies of incense for temple rituals. No doubt the provincial rulers and their associates made fat profits from these deals.

Extension of power meant delegation of authority. Possibly there was the traditional conflict between the 'man on the spot' – the efficient frontier soldier who knew local conditions – and the well-cushioned civil servants who issued the king's orders from his luxurious capital hundreds of miles away. So in time the provincial governors, the nomarchs, assumed greater independence. When their power could no longer be effectively restrained by a central authority it inevitably grew, until a time came when the nomarchs ruled almost as little kings – or, indeed, when the king was himself little more than another nomarch. It is significant that after a time these provincial officials no longer built their tombs alongside the royal pyramid as their forefathers had done, but in their own nomes.

In addition, these men of lesser rank more and more assumed for themselves the privilege, once reserved exclusively for Pharaoh, of joining the gods in afterlife, of becoming an Osiris in the next world. From royal tombs they adopted the painted offerings and magic spells that guaranteed this blessed eternity. The belief that any man who could afford the necessary tomb trappings might take a favoured place in the hereafter was never renounced; subsequently, indeed, all Egyptians assumed this comforting privilege. The cult of Osiris had to do largely with life after death and its rising popularity in no way challenged that of other deities. The 'democratization' of religion in which this resulted, however, marked a profound change in the Egyptian outlook.

It was in association with the growth of this cult of the god of the dead that, during these years, there were introduced statuettes known as shawabtys, which represented the deceased in miniature, not as he appeared in life, but as a wrapped mummy. Osiris and his wife Isis play a prominent part in the offering formulas with which these little mummiform figures were inscribed. Their original and primary function was to provide an alternative haven for the spirit in the event the actual mummy were by some chance destroyed. In time, however, this conception was expanded and the shawabty gradually assumed the nature of a magic servant who took over for

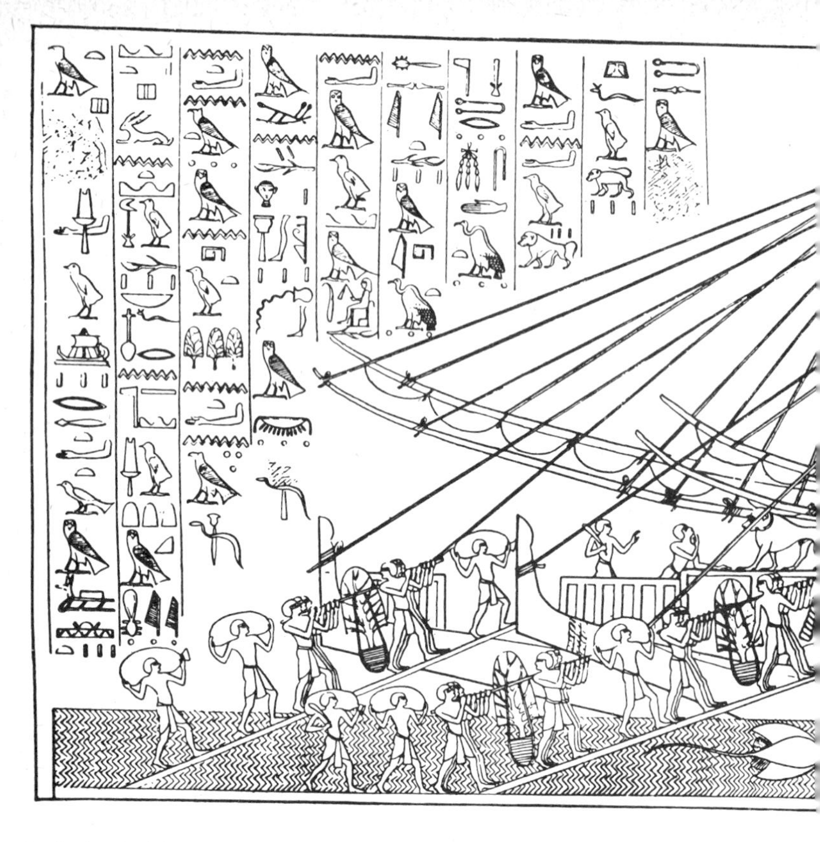

In the land of Punt, Egyptian traders load their ships with myrrh trees and incense; their cargo also includes several apes, who can be seen perched on the deck of one vessel. The trees were destined for Hatshepsut's temple (see page 97).

the deceased all the arduous and distasteful chores that might be demanded of him by the gods in the hereafter. Ultimately these statuettes almost completely replaced the representations of real servants that were such a common feature of earlier tombs; they enjoyed a widespread popularity that endured throughout the remainder of ancient Egyptian history.

Under the conditions described above, enterprising upstarts could flourish and grow rich, threatening the authority of those who owed their positions to birth and succession. This

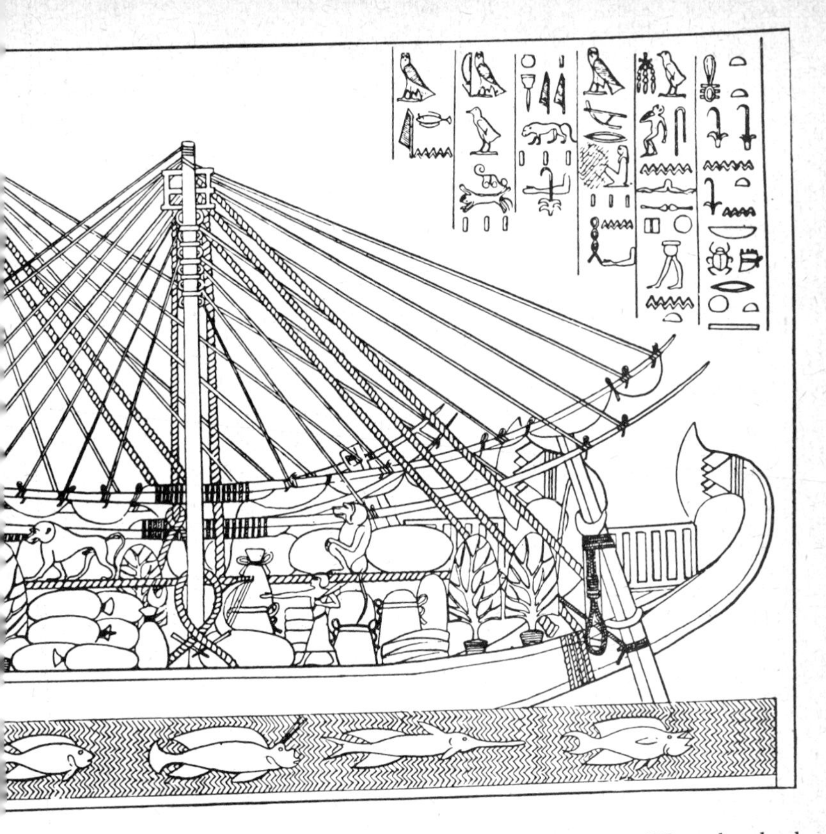

would account for Ipuwer's sour comment, 'He who had nothing is now rich, and the high official must court the parvenu.' His warning to the pharaoh evidently was to no avail, for the great Memphite kingdom founded by Narmer went down in ruin, never to rise again. The Heliopolitan priests of Re – who for more than five hundred years had so influenced the Memphite kings that many of them, such as Sahure and Niuserre, incorporated the god's name in their own – had to accept an amalgamation of their god with a minor deity named Amen, whose centre was the hitherto obscure town of Thebes in Upper Egypt.

For it was from Thebes (then called No-Amen) that there arose a new dynastic line of pharaohs, originally provincial nomarchs who by prowess in battle won the right to rule a

Horus, the falcon who ruled the heavens, enfolds Chephren in his wings.

reunited Egypt. Thus began Egypt's Second Golden Age, which historians call the Middle Kingdom (2133–1625 B.C.), ruled by the kings of the Eleventh and Twelfth Dynasties. It was during the long reign of Mentuhotep II, one of Egypt's great kings, that Thebes was firmly established as the seat of royal power. On the walls of a chapel at Dendera an inscription tells of him 'clubbing the eastern lands, striking down the hill countries, trampling the deserts, enslaving the Nubians . . . the Medjay and Wawat, the Libyans, and the (Asiatics)'. Mentuhotep was followed by such pharaohs as Sesostris I, Sesostris II, Sesostris III, and Ammenemes III, all men of force who maintained the supremacy of Thebes over the centuries to come.

The portrait sculptures of Middle Kingdom rulers present some striking differences from the royal portraiture of the Old Kingdom. Such Old Kingdom masterpieces as the figures of Chephren in the museum in Cairo and those of Mycerinus and his queen (see page 46) in the Boston Museum of Fine Arts have an aloof and imperturbable majesty that sets them above and apart from ordinary mortals. They are sure of their absolute authority. They are still men and women, but they have been idealized as muscular, ever-youthful figures beyond the touch of time. Some of the finest royal sculptures of the Middle Kingdom, particularly those of the Twelfth Dynasty, reflect more human concern. Sometimes they show the marks of age and suffering, notably in the case of Sesostris III. The likenesses of Ammenemes III show a hard, bitter, almost tortured face.

There were grim times as pharaohs of these dynasties struggled to re-establish the royal supremacy over rebellious nobles. As has been suggested, such sculptures may be 'evoking the angry spirits of these reformist kings'. Some of the writings of the period have a comparable bitterness. There is a document called 'The Teaching of King Ammenemes' (the first king of that name), who was apparently murdered by his court officers. In this work the dead king is made to advise his son, Sesostris I, 'Be on guard against subordinates. . . . Trust not a brother, know not a friend, and make not for thyself intimates.'

From these and other writings we can learn something about

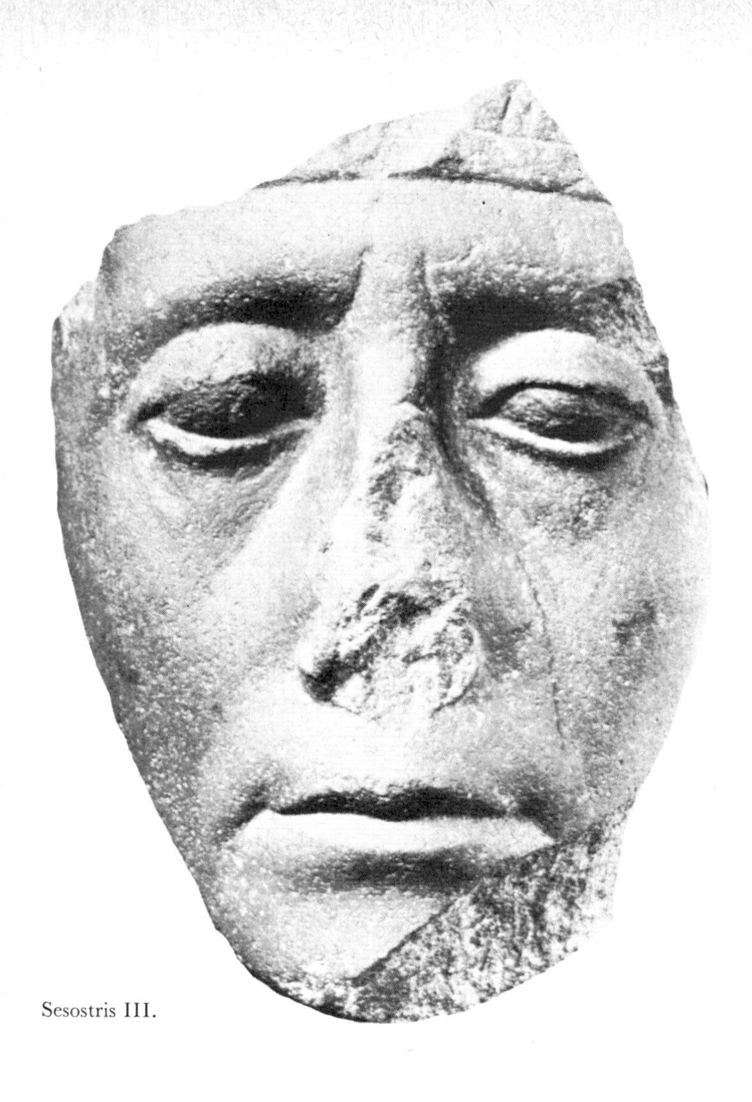

Sesostris III.

the achievements of the rulers of the Middle Kingdom. Some of them were remarkable men. The Ammenemes referred to above was an Upper Egyptian nobleman who seized power and overcame the hostile factions that were contending within the country at the close of the Eleventh Dynasty. The son to whom the cynical advice was addressed pushed the Egyptian frontier southward into Nubia. Ammenemes II was active in

Sinai, where he reopened and exploited the gold mines. Sesostris III, he of the careworn likeness, completely broke the resistance of the landed nobility. It was he who cut a vast channel for his war galleys through the granite of the First Cataract and completely subjugated Nubia. Egypt was begining to thrust out beyond her traditional frontiers and even to invade Syria for the first time.

We have only fragments from the literature that was produced during these centuries of trial and achievement. Among them, fortunately, is a minor masterpiece. It is not a work of fantasy, like the story of Snofru and his rowing girls; nor is it a historical work, although it may contain elements of history. It is a novel, one of the earliest examples of this art form, that tells the story of an official, Sinuhe, 'Prince and Count', who was serving in Libya with the army of the young prince, Sesostris. When news reached the camp that the prince's father, the great Ammenemes I, had died, the heir to the throne 'flew' to the capital to protect his interests. Sinuhe, either because he feared that civil war would break out, or because he suspected a plot directed against him, decided to flee from the camp.

The army was operating against the Tehenu in the Western Desert where the Allied Armies fought in World War II. On hearing the news of the king's death, Sinuhe writes:

> ... was mine heart distraught ... trembling fell on all my limbs. I betook me thence leaping, to seek me a hiding place; I placed me between two bushes so as to sunder the road from its traveller.

Then he set off southward, following a route which anyone who knows Egypt north of Cairo can still follow today. He reached the Nile above the point where it branches out through the Delta, and there 'crossed over in a barge without a rudder'. Sinuhe evidently made the crossing near modern Cairo, for the manuscript mentions the Red Mountain which is not far from that city and contained quarries which are still worked today. From this point he made his way towards the frontier of Palestine.

> I gave a road to my feet northwards, and attained the Wall of the Prince [a frontier fortress] which had been made to repel the Asiatics.

I bowed me down in a thicket lest the watcher for the day on the wall should espy me.

At even tide I passed on, and when day dawned I reached Petny and halted on an island [in the Bitter Lake]. There . . . I fell down for thirst, I was parched, my throat burned, and I said: 'This is the taste of death.' Then I lifted up mine heart and gathered up my body, for I heard the sound of the lowing of cattle and descried Bedouins. The sheik among them, who had been in Egypt, recognized me. He gave me water and cooked milk for me, and I went with him to his tribe and they treated me kindly.

Through Sinuhe's eyes, or those of the unknown author of this tale, we see the refugee official fleeing northward into Syria. 'Land gave me to land,' he writes, 'I set forth from Byblos and I drew near to Kedemi and spent a year and a half there.' Eventually he met a Syrian chieftain, Amunenshy, one of the despised desert nomads who, after asking him the reason for the flight from Egypt and receiving a noncommittal reply, persuaded Sinuhe to join his tribe. Then follows the most intriguing part of the tale. The Egyptian official, a highly civilized man educated at the court of the pharaoh, 'goes native'; he becomes one the scorned barbarians, and even marries the chief's daughter and has children by her. He rises to high rank and serves Amunenshy in peace and war.

One of the most dramatic episodes describes how Sinuhe fights 'a mighty man of Retenu' and defeats him. Sinuhe's description of his single combat with his adversary is not marred by understatement; it concludes:

. . . I avoided his arrows, one closely following the other, to the last arrow. Then he charged me, and I shot him, my arrow sticking in his neck. He cried out and fell on his nose. I laid him low with his own axe, and raised my shout of victory on his back. . . .

As the years pass Sinuhe is seized with longing to return to his own land and finally plucks up courage to write to Sesostris, formerly the prince whom he had served, whose camp he had deserted, and who had for many years occupied the throne of Egypt. The pharaoh, now a man advanced in years and presumably willing to forget and forgive former injuries, real or imagined, replies to Sinuhe's letter in kindly fashion, and the long-absent 'Prince and Count' makes the journey back to his distant homeland, dirty, and still wearing the dress of the desert tribes. He fearfully prostrates himself before the king, who calls out to his queen and the royal children:

> 'See, this is Sinuhe, who has come back as an Asiatic, a real son of the Bedouins.' She uttered an exceedingly loud cry, and the royal children shrieked out all together. They said unto his majesty: 'Is it not he in sooth?' [And] his majesty said: 'It is he . . .'

The story has a happy ending.

> Years were made to pass away from my body [Sinuhe remarks]. I was shaved, my hair was combed. A load of vermin was given over to the desert, and the [filthy] clothes of the nomads. And I was arrayed in finest linen and anointed with the best oil. I slept on a bed, and gave up the sand to those who live there, and the olive oil to him that smeareth himself therewith.

Sinuhe was given a house and servants, but, even more important to an Egyptian, a fine tomb was prepared for him:

> The chief architect began the building of it, the painter designed in it, the master sculptor carved in it, then superintendents of the necropolis busied themselves with it. All the glistening gear that is placed in a tomb-chamber, care was taken to place them into mine. . . . It was his majesty who caused it to be made. . . . And so live I, rewarded by the king, until the day of my death cometh.

No one has found Sinuhe's tomb, if indeed it ever existed. Aside from the works of the 'master painter' and the 'master sculptor' so generously provided by Sesostris, its equipment might well have included a collection of small, painted wood models of Sinuhe and of his servants busy at their various tasks. Such miniature figures, carved and coloured in the most realistic manner to represent the details of daily life as a favoured noble would have known it, were made in profusion during the Middle Kingdom. They were, like the paintings and reliefs earlier described, magical substitutes for the real thing, designed to serve the needs of the dead man in the life to come. Many of them have survived and may be seen in museums throughout the world. The finest assemblage of all was discovered by Herbert Winlock in 1920 when he was conducting for the Metropolitan Museum excavations in the necropolis at Thebes.

The tomb with which Winlock was concerned was that of a Middle Kingdom noble Meketre; it had been thoroughly plundered in antiquity and nothing remained of the body and its furniture. Winlock, an experienced Egyptologist, was well aware of this fact, so that he was unimpressed when one of his excited workmen overtook him with the words: 'The headman Hamid says I must tell no one, but Your Honour will see something up there.'

The same night, however, he was persuaded to return to the lonely tomb, hollowed in the hillside, and there saw something which few men have ever seen. Shining his torch into a hole in the rock he started back in astonishment and wonder.

> The beam of light [he wrote] shot into a little world of four thousand years ago, and I was gazing down into the midst of a myriad of brightly painted little men going this way and that. A tall slender girl gazed across at me perfectly composed; a gang of little men with sticks in their upraised hands drove spotted oxen; rowers tugged at their oars on a fleet of boats, while one ship seemed foundering right in front of me with its bow balanced precariously in the air. And all of this busy going and coming was in uncanny silence, as though the distance back over the forty centuries I looked across was too great for even an echo to reach my ears.

By one of those miracles that happen all to infrequently, this distinguished American Egyptologist came upon an intact cache of models, made for the tomb of a high official, which chanced to have been overlooked by the robbers who plundered the tomb thousands of years ago.

> He himself [writes Winlock] had been buried in a gilded coffin and a sarcophagus of stone in a mortuary chamber deep down under the back of the corridor, where the thieves had destroyed everything ages before our day. Only this little chamber had escaped and it was turning out to be a sort of secret closet where the provision was stored for the future life of the great man.

The little rock-cut chamber was crammed with models, all carefully made and proportioned; there were models of ships, ranging from a travelling boat with the model crew raising and

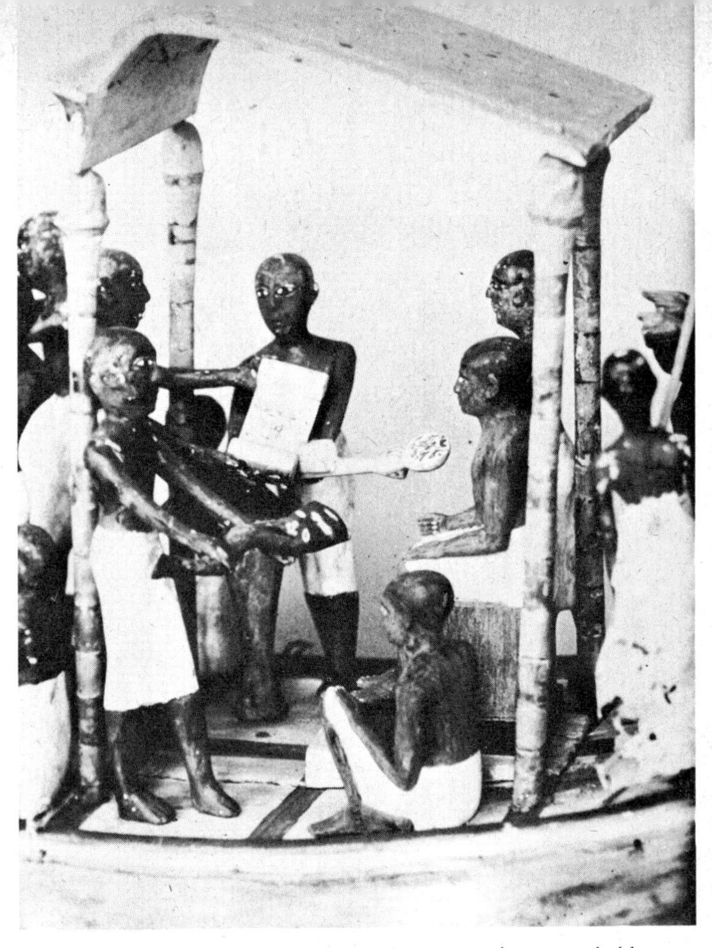

Holding their offerings out before them, three men who are probably priests present Meketre with a censer, a leg of beef, and a papyrus roll, which he will use in the afterworld. Written on the roll is a record of Meketre's funerary supplies: 'a thousand of bread and beer, a thousand of beef and fowl'.

trimming the sail and another with oars laid up in the oarlocks, to smaller craft with cooks at work which Winlock called kitchen tenders. These evidently followed the bigger craft and their function was to provide meals for the great man and his staff on their journey along the Nile. Then there were several models of fast yachts for less formal occasions; sporting boats for hunting, and fishing canoes.

Meketre appears seated under a canopy with a youth, perhaps his son, sitting beside him. While one of the crew poles the boat away from shore, others can be seen working the rudders, and hoisting a sail that has now disappeared.

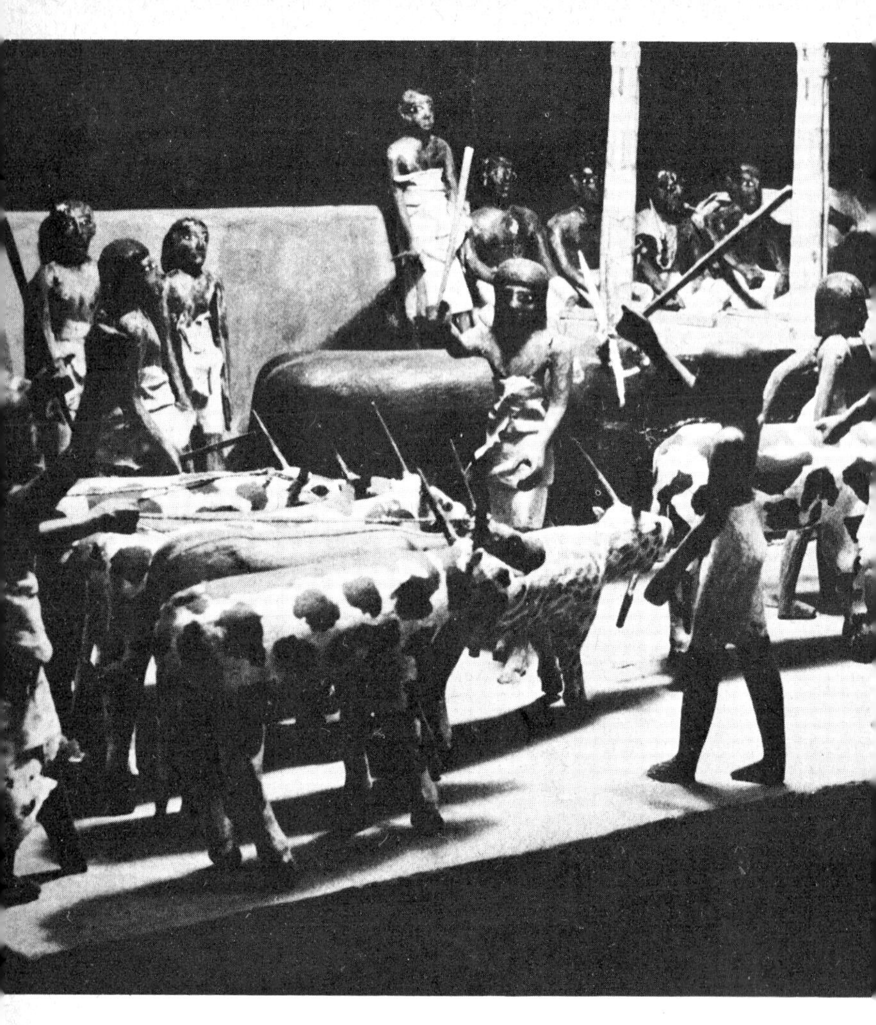

There were models of Meketre's residence, with its pillared courtyard and trees surrounding an ornamental pool. Another model showed Meketre inspecting his cattle, which were being driven past him as he sat beneath a pillared pavilion. There was a model stable for his cattle, a butcher's shop, a granary, a brewery, and a bakery, a weaving shop, a carpenter's shop – all teeming with tiny figures of the men and women who had served Meketre in life.

Meketre, watching estate workmen driving cattle past during an annual tax inspection. Seated within the pavilion, Meketre and his scribes have close-cropped hair as a sign of rank; the hair of the herdsmen grows long, to protect them from the sun.

By several lucky accidents there have also survived from the Middle Kingdom superb examples of the jewellery that was lavished by the pharaohs on their female relatives. The discovery of these long-buried treasures was doubly fortunate, for the court jewellers of the Twelfth Dynasty brought this ancient craft to an unsurpassed height of excellence.

The pyramid-building kings of both the Old and Middle Kingdoms constructed smaller pyramids for their wives alongside their own great buildings. In 1894–5 the archaeologist Jacques de Morgan, excavating near the pyramid of Sesostris III at Dashur, came upon a rock-cut gallery entered from a pit at the north-east corner of the main pyramid. This had belonged to one of the small subsidiary pyramids, and though it had been robbed of its main contents – the body and its furniture – de Morgan found a rectangular cavity at the foot of the sarcophagus. In this box, overlooked by the robbers, were jewellery and treasures of gold, silver, and semi-precious stones, mingled with fragments of the casket that had once enclosed them.

Not long afterwards de Morgan came upon other royal treasures belonging to royal ladies of the Twelfth Dynasty – Princess Merit, Princess Nubhotep, and the Princesses Ita and Khnumit. There were diadems, one with a naturalistic design of tendrils held together with florets of gold with hearts of carnelian, petals and berries of lapis lazuli; there were pectorals, or breast ornaments, of gold, one with the cartouch of Sesostris II and another with that of Sesostris III.

Nineteen years later Petrie, excavating near the ruined pyramid of Sesostris II, found an equally wonderful cache. In one of the smaller royal tombs a recess at the side of the ransacked sarcophagus chamber had been choked by dried mud left by flood water in very ancient times, and under this cover the jewellery had escaped detection. These objects, among the finest known examples of ancient Egyptian goldwork, had belonged to Princess Sathathorynet, daughter of one pharaoh, sister of another, and aunt of a third.

Among these treasures were a silver mirror, toilet vases containing perfumed ointments, and even small copper razors. There was a girdle made of hollow golden shells in the form of lion heads, and joined by double rows of amethyst beads, a girdle so small that only a very slim woman could have worn it; and – an intriguing detail – the little golden shells of which it was composed contained pellets which would make a tinkling sound when the princess walked.

From the tombs of the royal masters whose bounty provided such precious gifts, little has survived. In emulation of past monarchs they too built pyramids, at Dashur, Hawara, and Lisht; magnificent buildings in themselves, though inferior to

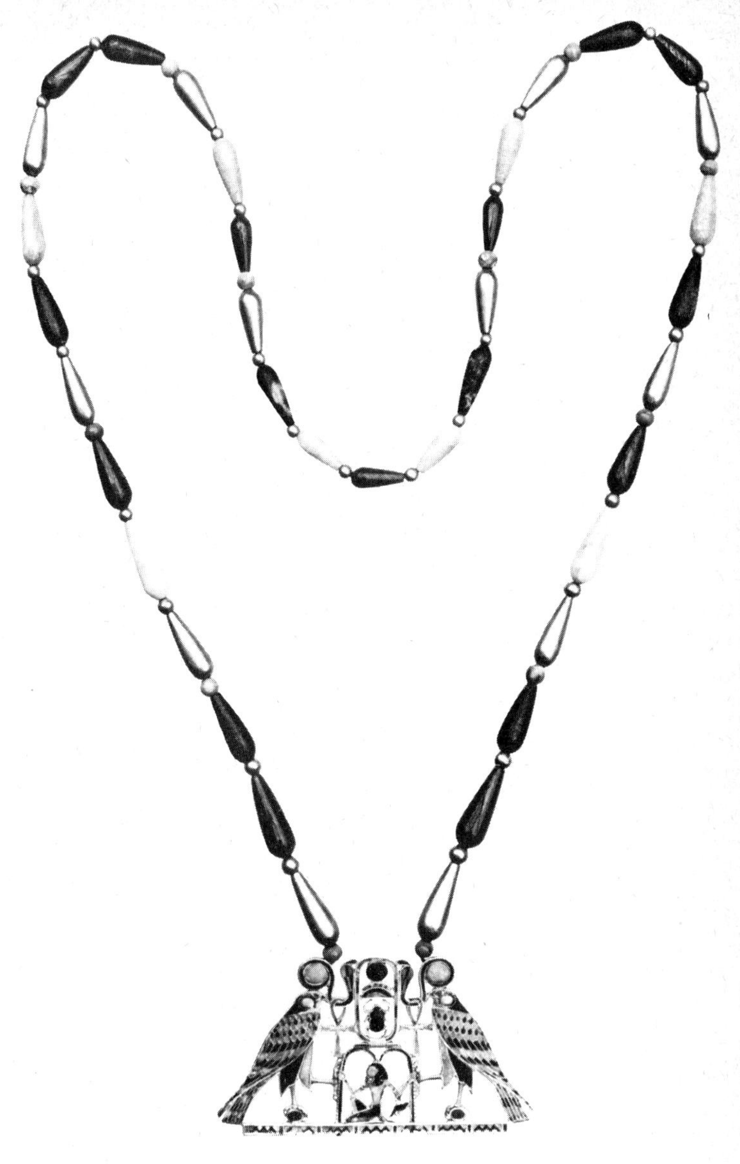

This inlaid golden pectoral, part of the treasure of a Middle Kingdom princess, displays a figure of the god of years, promising her father, the king, hundreds of thousands of years of life.

those of the Fourth Dynasty. The over-all design of these tombs was the same, but the architects had thought of new devices to confuse their eternal enemy, the tomb robber. Mere masses of masonry were no longer enough. Deep shafts in the rock had failed, as had the chambers within Cheops' Great Pyramid, built within the main structure and sealed by ponderous portcullis blocks of granite. The architects of the Middle Kingdom tried these and still other methods. One of the two pyramids built for Ammenemes III incorporated puzzle passages of elaborate intricacy designed to outwit plunderers; blind alleys that led in various directions; trap doors that opened the way to other dead ends; and, concealed in the roof of one passage, a twenty-ton block of stone that could slide sideways, leading on to other chambers and corridors and eventually to still another dead end.

All this ingenuity, skill, knowledge, and labour were wasted. As usual, intruders found the true sepulchre, robbed it, took away its most valuable contents, and destroyed the rest. When Petrie tunnelled his way in some four thousand years later, he found only an empty water-logged room choked with mud and debris.

Among the pharaohs of the Middle Kingdom there were, as we have seen men of great stature. But the most powerful of them never enjoyed the absolute authority that had been exercised by Old Kingdom rulers. With the end of the reign of Ammenemes III this second great period of Egyptian history showed signs of disintegration. The traditional life of the land went on as before. The great river rose and then fell, the crops were gathered, labourers and craftsmen went about their accustomed tasks in the ways of their ancestors. But there were indications of new turmoil in the Delta. This, the richest area in Egypt, lay nearest the several foreign lands whose inhabitants, in times of unrest, were ever tempted to move in and settle on this good earth.

3 · Glory and Decline

According to Manetho, the Middle Kingdom was brought to an end by an invasion of Asiatic tribes whose leaders he called the Hyksos, a term derived from an Egyptian expression that may be translated 'Rulers of the Desert Uplands', or 'Rulers of the Upland-dwellers'. These 'upland-dwellers' were tribes from Palestine, Lebanon, and Syria, some of whom were Semitic and may have included ancestors of the Hebrews. Actually this was no sudden invasion, but rather a successful takeover bid by peoples who had already infiltrated into the Delta area and had been settled in this northern part of Egypt for generations. Such people had been in the habit of coming to Egypt, especially in times of famine or drought in their own homelands, perhaps selling some of their number into servitude in return for corn. Some, as we know from the much later Old Testament story of Joseph and his brethren, held positions of high trust.

They were a lively-minded, intelligent, energetic people; moreover they provided a link with the world of western Asia, and brought with them innovations from that world which were to have a great influence on the conservative, valley-dwelling Egyptians. Among these were the use of bronze for implements and for new kinds of swords and daggers, and the powerful composite bow; also the horse, the wheel (almost unknown to the Egyptians before this period), and, in conjunction, the horse-drawn war chariot.

It may have been the possession of superior weapons, among other factors, which tempted them to exploit the weakness and dissension among Egypt's rulers and seize power in the Delta area and, later, to extend a loose suzerainty over the native Egyptian rulers who still nominally controlled Middle Egypt from Thebes. The Hyksos also entered into alliance with the rulers of Kush (Nubia), who by this time had broken away

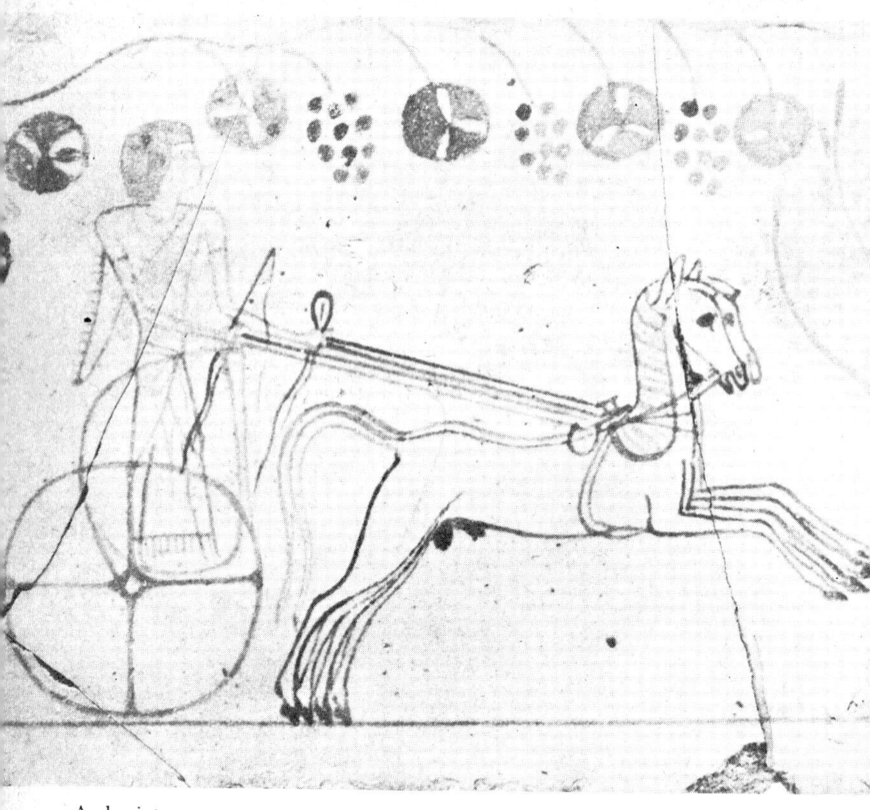

A chariot.

from Thebes; thus the Theban kings were hemmed in to north and south.

During this so-called Second Intermediate Period (1786–1567 B.C.) the Hyksos kings, ruling from Avaris in the eastern Delta, adopted pharaonic titles and customs; but often their outlandish names – Khyan, Anat-her, Pachnan – reveal Semitic origins. (The most intriguing of these names, found on scarabs of the period, is Yakubher which can very probably be identified with the name of the patriarch Jacob.) Something had happened in Egypt which had never happened before. In the past there had been civil wars and frontier battles, but during its already long history Egypt had never known the ignominy of foreign occupation, of alien pretenders to Pharaoh's throne.

It is easy to denigrate the ancient Egyptians for their conservatism and insularity. Yet there must have been more in what we label Egyptian culture than an elaborate governmental hierarchy, a viable economic system, and a tenacious religious tradition; it was a way of life which Egyptians valued sufficiently to fight for. During the late years of this Intermediate Period they turned on the foreign intruders with what might be called patriotic fervour. From the Asiatic settlers the Egyptians had learned much. They now proceeded to use the practical, technical innovations they had borrowed from these aliens in order to reunite the entire valley of the Nile under the sovereignty of native rulers.

The Theban prince Sekenenre is credited with being the ruler who began driving out the foreign intruders, a process followed up with increasing effect by his successors Kamose and Ahmose. Sekenenre's mummified body was among those found in a cache at Deir el Bahri in 1881. The body was twisted as if in agony, and the skull and neck bore hideous wounds. He may well have been killed in battle, fighting the Hyksos; there is documentary proof that both he and Kamose did indeed lead a campaign against the hated Asiatics.

An inscribed stele of Kamose, discovered as recently as 1954 at Thebes, completes the story told in a document discovered earlier. The following brief extract describes the Theban ruler's northward advance.

I fared downstream in might to overthrow the Asiatics by the command of Amen, the just of counsels; my brave army in front of me like a breath of fire, troops of Medja-Nubians [mercenary soldiers] aloft upon our cabins to spy out the Setyu and to destroy their places. East and west were in possession of their fat and the army was supplied with things everywhere.

There is in this report of Kamose's campaign a militant zest which foreshadows that of the greater kings who were to follow – men such as Tuthmosis III and Ramesses II.

I spent the night in my ship, my heart happy [the account continues]. When the earth became light, I was upon him [an Egyptian collaborationist] as it were a hawk. The time of perfuming the mouth [the midday meal] came, and I overthrew him, I razed his wall, I slew his people, and I caused his wife to go down to the river bank. My soldiers were like lions with their prey, with serfs, cattle, milk, fat and honey, dividing up their possessions. . . . Your heart is undone, base Asiatic, who used to say 'I am lord, and there is none equal to me from Khmun and Pi-hathor down to Avaris.'

The document goes on to describe how Kamose intercepts a letter passing between the Hyksos king and his ally, the ruler of Kush, whom he had corrupted and persuaded to turn against his natural lord.

I captured a messenger of his high up over the Oasis travelling southward to Kush for the sake of a written dispatch, and I found upon it this message in writing from the chieftain of Avaris. . . . 'Why have you arisen as chieftain without letting me know? Have you (not) beheld what Egypt has done against me, the chieftain who is in it, Kamose the Mighty, ousting me from my soil, and I have not reached him . . .'

In about 1567 B.C. when Ahmose, Kamose's younger brother, succeeded to the throne and founded the Eighteenth Dynasty, Egyptian civilization was already more than fifteen hundred years old, three times the age of either the Greek or Roman civilizations in their prime. Our western democratic system – which its harsher critics believe to be already in decline – has a very much briefer history. Yet with Ahmose's reign Egypt entered a period of unprecedented brilliance, known to us as the New Kingdom, which, though the traditional pattern of civilization continued, saw Egypt established as the greatest and richest power on earth.

Having pushed the 'upland-dwellers' out of the Delta, the kings of the Eighteenth Dynasty proceeded to carry Egyptian conquest far into the homelands of their enemies, for they realized that it was not enough merely to close and guard the frontiers. Unless the Asiatics were pursued and subdued they would reorganize and return. So the Egyptians became conquerors and colonizers. For the first time scores of thousands of Egyptians saw the countries that lay outside their sheltered valley; lands where there were mountains more than nine thousand feet high, where there was 'a Nile in the sky' (rain) and a river (the Euphrates) that 'in running southwards runs northwards'. Here the scribes tried to explain to their compatriots the course of a river that unlike the Nile, the father of all rivers, flowed from north to south instead of vice versa.

The Egyptians became soldiers; not conscripts recruited for brief periods, but veteran professionals one of whom (according to a popular literary composition of the New Kingdom) could write to a young and boastful colleague:

> You are a *mahir* [a hero], who is skilled in deeds of valour! A *mahir*, such as you are, is qualified to march at the head of the host! Forward, O *maryen*, to shoot! Behold, there is the [ambuscade] in a ravine two thousand cubits deep, filled with boulders and shingle. You make a detour. You grasp the bow . . . you let the chieftains see what is pleasing to their eyes until your hand grows weary. . . .

At this point, the old warrior even puts in a few Canaanite words, which is like a veteran of the Pacific war quoting a few words of Malay or Japanese.

> Behold, there is the narrow defile [he goes on] made perilous by Bedouins, who are hidden beneath the bushes; some of them are of four cubits and five cubits from the nose unto the sole of the foot [a typical old soldier's exaggeration; this would have made them seven to nine feet tall], fierce of face, their heart not mild. . . .

Then the author describes the plight of the *mahir*, a green young chariot officer, when he is caught in the narrow defile, with

> the ravine . . . on one side of you, the mountain rises on the other. On you go and guide your chariot beside you. . . . You unharness the horse, in order to repair the hand [evidently a part of the chariot] . . . you are not expert in the way of binding it, and you don't know how to fasten it together. The . . . [some other part of the chariot] falls from its place, and the horse is already too heavily laden to load him with it. You are sick at heart and start to go on foot . . . you fancy that the enemy is behind you. Then trembling takes hold of you. Ah, would that you had a hedge (between you and the other side)! Your horse is galled up to the time that you find quarters for the night. Now you know what pain tastes like.

And there were other hazards, not unfamiliar to the modern soldier. At a later stage the *mahir* encounters a girl, a fair maiden who keeps watch over the vineyards. She takes you to herself as companion and shows you the colour of her bosom. You are recognized [by the enemy] . . . and put on trial, and your tunic of good Upper Egyptian linen, you sell [as a bribe to facilitate escape] . . . You sleep every evening with a piece of woollen cloth about you, you slumber and are inert. They [steal] your bow, your knife, your quiver, and your reins are cut in the darkness.

Your horse is gone. . . . The road stretches out before you. The chariot is smashed . . . your weapons fall to the ground and are buried in the sand. . . .

And so on; possibly an exaggeration, but the writer of that satire, who died some three thousand years ago, has said enough to make it clear that ancient Egyptian soldiers of the New Kingdom were fully familiar with the hazards of campaigning in a strange and hostile country.

A succession of pharaohs of the Eighteenth Dynasty extended Egypt's conquests far into Syria. The greatest of these was Tuthmosis III who finally rid himself of his detested stepmother, Hatshepsut, who had ruled as a pharaoh for twenty years. (We do not know what may have happened to this dominating female; she simply disappears from the records.) By his own boast Tuthmosis III was 'the smiter of the rulers of foreign countries who had attacked him'. It is recorded that he fought at least seventeen successful campaigns, the most extensive of which carried him beyond the Euphrates River. After each victory he returned to his capital at Thebes, bearing the spoils of war to lay before the Theban god Amen-Re. The god was well pleased with his all-conquering son and, in a famous paean inscribed on one of the temple walls, praised the pharaoh in grandiose terms:

Come thou to me, rejoicing to see my beauty, O my son, my champion, Tuthmosis. . . .
I give unto thee valour and victory over every land;
I place thy might and the fear of thee in all lands,
And the terror of thee as far as the four supports of the sky. . . .
The chiefs of all lands are united in thy grasp –
I stretch forth mine own hands to bind them for thee;
I bind the Nubian Bedouin in ten thousands and thousands, and the northern peoples in hundred thousands.

Tuthmosis III pours a libation before the throne of Amen.

I cast thine enemies beneath thy sandals, and thou destroyest the recalcitrant,
Even as I have committed unto thee the earth in its length and in its breadth,
While the Western peoples and the Easterners are under thy control.
Thou treadest every foreign land with joyful heart, and none ventureth himself in thy vicinity;
But as I am thy guide, so thou reachest out unto them. . . .

I cause them to see thy majesty as a fierce lion: thou makest them into corpses throughout their valleys.
I have come to cause thee to trample the tail of the world; that which the sea encircleth is enclosed in thy grasp.
I cause them to see thy majesty as a soaring falcon that taketh what it perceiveth according to its desire.

I have come to cause thee to trample those who dwell at the head of the world; thou bindest the sand-dwellers in captivity.
I cause them to see thy majesty as an Upper Egyptian jackal swift of feet, the runner that prowleth throughout the Two Lands.

I have come to cause thee to trample the Nubians; everything is in thy grasp as far as Shatiu-djeba.
I cause them to see thy majesty like thy two brothers [Horus and Seth], whose arms I have joined with thee in victory.

On the walls of the temple, also, Tuthmosis is depicted wielding a mace and grasping the hair of his Asiatic enemies, almost exactly as Narmer was shown seventeen hundred years earlier on his commemorative slate palette. The only important difference occurs in the scale. The palette is less than two feet long; the temple of Amen-Re at Karnak rises to a height of more than one hundred feet. The idea behind both scenes is the same, and nothing more clearly suggests the essential conservatism of the Egyptian outlook.

To celebrate his victorious reign Tuthmosis caused to be erected from time to time commemorative obelisks, in accordance with old tradition. The subsequent travels of four of these monuments, proclaiming the might of this great conquerer, are memorable in themselves: one now stands in the Hippodrome at Istanbul; a second was erected during the Renaissance in the piazza of St John Lateran in Rome; another stands on the Thames Embankment in London; and the fourth, a gift of Egyptians to the United States, towers beside the Metropolitan Museum in New York's Central Park.

The foreign campaigns of Tuthmosis brought wealth pouring into Egypt in the form of gold and other precious metals; captives to serve as mercenaries and to work in bondage on the projects of the pharaoh and his nobles; horses, cattle, and other animals in great quantities; and above all regular tribute from the newly established colonies and satellites. Not all this new wealth came from conquest, however; there were increased trading contacts, and in some of the Theban tombs we see paintings of embassies from as far away as the island of Crete, bringing the products of their lands in exchange for Egyptian goods.

Egypt experienced increasing influences from foreign lands. Sons of Syrian princes were brought to Thebes as hostages, educated at the Egyptian court, and sent back to govern their own lands as Egyptian vassals. Princesses from foreign lands married into the royal and noble families, or were added to the harems of such households. Amenhotep III, the luxury-loving pharaoh who spent his life enjoying the fruits of his predecessors' conquests, added Mitannian princesses to his international assemblage of wives and favourites. When local medical help failed him in his illness, he asked the king of Mitanni for

Amenhotep III.

A sculptor's preliminary study of Akhenaten.

a statue of the Ninevite goddess of love, Ishtar, hoping that her celebrated healing powers would relieve his symptoms.

His son, Amenhotep IV, the so-called heretic king, initiated a short-lived religious revolution, the philosophical content of which is still a matter of discussion. Some believe the king was mad, or at least mentally unbalanced; others, like James Henry Breasted, have called him 'the first individual in history', a man who had the courage to defy the powerfully entrenched priesthood of Amen-Re, and with his beautiful wife Nefretiti to establish a new capital at el Amarna, where he devoted his life to teaching a novel religion. This was based on the worship of the Aten, the 'One God', whose symbol was the sun's disk. The pharaoh changed his name to Akhenaten, meaning 'he who is serviceable to Aten'. In a single stroke he tried to abolish the innumerable deities whom the Egyptians had inherited from predynastic times; all were to be swept away, even Osiris, god of the dead, who by this time had almost come to equal Amen-Re in importance. This religious revolt was accompanied by an equally short-lived revolution in art; the statuary and tomb reliefs of the so-called Amarna period, of which the best known is the Berlin portrait bust of Nefretiti, are distinguished by a startling realism that contrasted sharply with the traditional canons of Egyptian art. Akhenaten encouraged his sculptors to depict him as he really was, with swollen belly,

Queen Nefretiti.

Akhenaten and Nefretiti playing with their daughters under the rays of the sun.

elongated jaw, and pronounced effeminate characteristics; also to show him, not in the conventional austere pose of the god-king, but, with informality, as a devoted spouse and parent, kissing and fondling his infant daughters (he had no sons).

The Hymn to Aten, which is attributed to the heretic pharaoh and which is inscribed on the walls of several tombs near his capital, contains passages of lyrical beauty; the sun is not merely the fierce, all-pervading heat, driving men into the shade of midday, but the gentle source of life in all created things.

Thou appearest beautifully on the horizon of heaven,
Thou living Aten, the beginning of life!
When thou art risen on the eastern horizon,
Thou hast filled every land with thy beauty.
Thou art gracious, great, glistening, and high over every land;
Thy rays encompass the lands to . . . all that thou hast made:
As thou art Re, thou reachest to the end of them;
(Thou) subduest them (for) thy beloved son.
Though thou art far away, thy rays are on earth;
Though thou art in their faces, no one knows thy going.

When thou settest in the western horizon,
The land is in darkness, in the manner of death.
They sleep in a room, with heads wrapped up,
Nor sees one eye the other.
All their goods which are under their heads might be stolen,
(But) they would not perceive (it).
Every lion is come forth from his den;
All creeping things, they sting.
Darkness is a shroud, and the earth is in stillness,
For he who made them rests in his horizon.

At daybreak, when thou arisest on the horizon,
When thou shinest as the Aten by day,
Thou drivest away the darkness and givest thy rays.
The Two Lands are in festivity every day,
Awake and standing upon (their) feet,
For thou hast raised them up.
Washing their bodies, taking (their) clothing,
Their arms are (raised) in praise at thy appearance.
All the world, they do their work.

All beasts are content with their pasturage;
Trees and plants are flourishing.
The birds which fly from their nests,
Their wings are (stretched out) in praise to thy *ka*.
All beasts spring upon (their) feet.
Whatever flies and alights,
They live when thou hast risen (for) them.
The ships are sailing north and south as well,
For every way is open at thy appearance.
The fish in the river dart before thy face;
Thy rays are in the midst of the great green sea.

Creator of seed in woman,
Thou who makest fluid into man,
Who maintainest the son in the womb of his mother,
Who soothest him with that which stills his weeping,
Thou nurse (even) in the womb,
Who givest breath to sustain all that he has made!
When he descends from the womb to breathe
On the day when he is born,
Thou openest his mouth completely,
Thou suppliest his necessities.
When the chick in the egg speaks within the shell,
Thou givest him breath within it to maintain him.
When thou hast made him his fulfilment within the egg, to
  break it,
He comes forth from the egg to speak at his completed (time);
He walks upon his legs when he comes forth from it.

How manifold it is, what thou hast made!
They are hidden from the face (of man),
O sole god, like whom there is no other!
Thou didst create the world according to thy desire,
Whilst thou wert alone:
All men, cattle, and wild beasts,
Whatever is on earth, going upon (its) feet,
And what is on high, flying with its wings.

Thy rays suckle every meadow.
When thou risest, they live, they grow for thee.
Thou makest the seasons in order to rear all that thou hast made,
The winter to cool them,
And the heat that they may taste thee.
Thou hast made the distant sky in order to rise therein,
In order to see all that thou dost make.
Whilst thou wert alone,
Rising in thy form as the living Aten,
Appearing, shining, withdrawing, or approaching,
Thou madest millions of forms of thyself alone.
Cities, towns, fields, road, and river –
Every eye beholds thee over against them,

Eighteenth Dynasty painting showing [above] fish being speared and (below) the harvest in a vineyard, with farm workers trampling upon the grapes. In the lowest register, peasants net water birds in the marshes, and clean their catch for the table.

For thou art the Aten of the day over the earth. . . .

Thou art in my heart,
And there is no other that knows thee
Save thy son Neferkheperure Waenre,
For thou hast made him well versed in thy plans and in thy strength.
The world came into being by thy hand,
According as thou hast made them.
When thou hast risen they live,
When thou settest they die.
Thou art lifetime thy own self,
For one lives (only) through thee.
Eyes are (fixed) on beauty until thou settest.
All work is laid aside when thou settest in the west.
(But) when (thou) risest (again),
[Everything is] made to flourish for the king . . .
Since thou didst found the earth
And raise them up for the son,
Who came forth from thy body:
the King of Upper and Lower Egypt . . . Akhenaten . . .
and the Chief Wife of the King . . . Nefretiti, living and
youthful for ever and ever.

There is a tenderness in this poem, which is far removed from the aggressiveness in the paean of Amen-Re, delighting in blood and conquest. Both in its content and in its structure it has often been compared with the 104th Psalm. Yet as critics have said, it contains no moral instructions, no system of ethics. It is doubtful if this new religion affected more than a minority of sophisticated courtiers. Most Egyptians probably continued to worship the traditional gods, even though the pharaoh in his fanaticism caused the name Amen-Re to be erased from every monument his agents could reach. When after less than forty years the royal heretic died, Egypt returned to her old familiar polytheism. In reaction to his reign, the name of Akhenaten was in turn removed from some of his monuments, and the temple dedicated to Aten, at Karnak, was completely destroyed. The Eighteenth Dynasty, which had begun gloriously under the warrior and liberator Ahmose, finally flickered out, leaving behind a legacy of idealistic pacifism, a neglected empire, and a powerful new enemy – the

Hittites of Asia Minor. These people, 'the abominable Kheta' as they were termed in one war-time manifesto, were pushing into Syria and terrorizing the remaining loyal Egyptian colonies into submission.

Among the few who stood out against the invader and remained faithful to Egypt was a certain Ribbadi, governor of Byblos, in Lebanon. By a fortunate chance his desperate appeals to Akhenaten, filed in the pharaoh's foreign office at el Amarna, have survived to tell their own story.

> Behold Aziru [king of Amurru, a region north of Lebanon, who was conspiring with the Hittites against the pharaoh] has fought my chiefs, and the chiefs whom I dispatched to the city Simyra he has caused to be seized in the city. Both the city Beruta [Beirut] and the city Ziouna are sending ships to the city. All who are in the land of the Amorites have gathered themselves . . . I need men to save the rebellion of this land . . . Give me soldiers!

And later, when the traitor Aziru, with the aid of his Hittite masters, had taken Simyra, Ribbadi wrote again to Akhenaten:

> Behold what has befallen the lands of the king on account of him; and he cried peace unto the land, and now behold what has befallen the city of Simyra – a station of my Lord [the pharaoh], a fortress . . . and they spoil our fortress . . . ah, the cries of the place . . . a violent man and a dog!

One's heart goes out to the old governor when one reads his last letter to the pacifist pharaoh, who passed on these appeals to his foreign office clerks, while consoling himself with the mysteries of his esoteric faith.

> March against him [implores Ribbadi]. . . . March against him and smite him . . . the land is the king's land [Egyptian territory]; and since I have talked thus and you have not moved, the city of Simyra has been lost. There is no money to buy horses; all is finished, we have been spoiled . . . give me thirty companies of horses with chariots . . . men, men . . . there is none of this for me . . . not a horse. . . .

And that is the last we hear from Ribbadi.

But it was not the end of Egypt's imperial claims. A new

dynasty of pharaohs, the Nineteenth, won back most of the territory lost through the indolence of Amenhotep III, Akhenaten, and their successors. There is something astounding and superb in the way this civilization, now almost two thousand years old, rose again to the call of destiny. Conservative and tradition-bound it may have been; but it was not effete. Monarchs such as Sethi I and Ramesses II recovered much of their Asian territory, and commemorated their exploits with inscriptions on the walls of the enlarged and beautified temple of Amen-Re at Karnak. Whatever the degree of his success, or lack of it, the campaigns of Pharaoh were always shown, by timeless convention, as absolute, complete, and personal triumphs. Ramesses II met the Hittites at Kadesh, in Syria, and fought a battle which, though inconclusive, he celebrated as a crushing victory for Pharaoh. In any event, this stand-off engagement resulted in a treaty which established a peace between these great empires that was never broken. Copies of the agreement signed by Ramesses II and the Hittite king, Hattusilis, have been preserved both at Thebes and at the Hittite capital of Boghazkoy in Asia Minor. Now they are no longer 'the abominable Kheta'. In the treaty Hattusilis is referred to as 'the great king . . . the valiant', in accordance with diplomatic usage of the day. Ramesses even took to himself a Hittite princess whom he found 'fair of face [like] a goddess . . . and he loved her more than anything'.

Less than a century later Ramesses III, of the Twentieth Dynasty, had to meet an even more deadly threat. In his reign (1198–1166 B.C.) there was a great movement of peoples throughout western Asia, Asia Minor, and the Aegean. It was the time when the Dorian invaders were pouring into Greece, dispersing the Mycenaeans; a time when the Hittites, so lately allied to Egypt, were being swept out of power in Asia Minor by new invaders; a time when not only armies but whole peoples – with their cattle, and baggage trains – were swarming down the eastern coast of the Mediterranean, seeking new and more promising lands in which to settle.

Ramesses III met them, at sea and on land, and hurled them back from the gates of Egypt. In the commemorative scenes which he ordered carved on his temple walls at Medinet

Habu we see the ships of one of these invading peoples, the biblical Philistines, rammed and sunk by the pharaoh's war galleys. One scene depicts an encounter between an Egyptian and a Philistine ship somewhere in the Nile Delta or the sea beyond it. From the crow's-nest of the Egyptian battleship an archer snipes at the deck of the Asiatic vessel. The Egyptian oarsmen, protected by high bulwarks, haul on their oars, while Egyptian marines hack, slash, and fire arrows at their enemies. This is one of the earliest representations of a naval conflict in the world; and it was a decisive battle. At the end of that day the drowned bodies of thousands – Asiatics and Egyptians – floated in the Nile swell, alongside the broken, derelict hulks of their vessels. And though the surviving invaders were able to cling to the sea coasts of Lebanon and Palestine, they did not dare attempt to enter Egypt again.

In Thebes the results of the imperial conquests were reflected in many significant ways – especially in architecture, tombs,

Hatshepsut's temple at Thebes.

and rich furnishings. The sepulchres of the Theban rulers during the Hyksos domination were handsome, but not particularly remarkable. But once Thebes had become the supreme capital of Egypt, it rose to a magnificence surpassing even that of Memphis, from which the Old Kingdom pharaohs had ruled a thousand years earlier. The Theban god Amen, originally a minor deity, had been amalgamated with the sun god Re as king of gods under the name Amen-Re, as we have seen. His temple at Karnak, enlarged and glorified by successive generations of pharaohs – the Tuthmosides, the Amenhoteps, and the Ramesside kings – became the largest religious building in the world, and no other built in subsequent times has exceeded it in size.

The Hypostyle Hall at Karnak, completed by Ramesses II, the most industrious builder of all the pharaohs. The capitals of its columns represent papyrus buds or umbels.

The Hypostyle Hall of this immense complex, the largest single chamber of any temple in the world, covers fifty-four thousand square feet, almost equal to the space occupied by one of the greatest cathedrals of medieval Europe – Canterbury in England. A number of its one hundred and thirty-four columns are twelve feet thick and sixty-nine feet high, each about the size of Trajan's column in Rome, and crowned by capitals of such size that one hundred men could stand upon them; the rest are forty-three feet high. But this many-columned hall was only the central feature of a building complex which would cover much of mid-Manhattan. Within the walls of the temple there would be room for St Peter's in Rome, the Milan Cathedral, and Notre Dame in Paris. The outer

Queen Teye came from a humble background, but she was chosen by Amenhotep III as his Great Royal Wife, taking precedence over all other women in the royal harem.

walls would comfortably enclose ten European cathedrals.

Stretching for miles along the east bank of the Nile were the palaces of the kings and the villas of the nobles, each enclosed within its walled gardens. Here also were the wharves crowded with goods from Asia, Crete, and the Aegean Islands. On the west bank lay other palaces, including that of Amenhotep III with the great pleasure lake he had had made virtually overnight for his favourite queen, Teye; here also was the necropolis, the City of the Dead, housing the mortal remains of kings and nobles. The pharaohs still made their Houses of Eternity in the West, where Re 'went to his horizon'. The mud-brick mastabas of the early dynastic period, the stone pyramids of the Old and Middle Kingdoms, all had failed to protect the embalmed and consecrated body of the king. So now the architects devised a new stratagem; pyramids were abandoned, and instead the kings were buried in rock-hewn chambers deep in the cliffs, approached by long, sloping corridors. All the pharaohs of the New Kingdom tunnelled their last resting places in the living rock of the Theban mountains, in a lonely defile beyond the eastern face of the cliff, the famous Valley of the Tombs of the Kings.

Every trick used by the tomb builders of the Middle Kingdom to thwart plunderers was employed, besides some new ones: 'puzzle-passages', deep pits in the floor of the corridor, blind alleys, and false burial chambers beyond which flights of stairs tunnelled still deeper through the rock to the final chamber. The tomb of Sethi I has several such devices; the tomb chambers of Hatshepsut extend for more than five hundred feet, starting high up in the Theban cliffs, the entrance obscure and difficult of access. But despite all these precautions the tomb robbers got through; aided, no doubt, by corrupt officials who hoped to get their percentage of the loot.

Documents have survived that report the trials of certain malefactors who were apprehended while pillaging the sepulchres of earlier kings.

We went to rob the tombs in accordance with our regular habit [the culprit explained to his inquisitors] and we found the pyramid of King Sekhemreshedtaui, the son of Re, Sebkemsaf, this being not at all like the pyramids and tombs of the nobles which we habitually went to rob. We took our copper tools and forced a way into the pyramid of this king through its innermost part. We found its underground chambers, and we took lighted candles in our hands and went down. Then we broke through the rubble that we found at the mouth of his recess, and found this god lying at the back of his burial place. And we found the burial place of Queen Nubkhas (his queen) situated beside him, it being protected and guarded by plaster and covered with rubble. This also we broke through, and found her resting [there] in like manner. We opened their sarcophagi and their coffins in which they were, and found the noble mummy of this king equipped with a falchion; a large number of amulets and jewels of gold were upon his neck, and his headpiece of gold was upon him. The noble mummy of this king was completely bedecked with gold, and his coffins were adorned with gold and silver inside and out and inlaid with all kinds of precious stones. We collected the gold we found on the noble mummy of this god, together with . . . his amulets and jewels which were on his neck and . . . the coffins in which he was resting [and we] found [the] queen in exactly the same state. We collected all that we found upon her likewise, and set fire to their coffins. We took their furniture which we found with them consisting of articles of gold, silver, and bronze, and divided them among ourselves.

That is the contemporary report of a court investigation which was made in Egypt some three thousand years ago. There had always been such looting, but in the Twentieth Dynasty it became epidemic. This was a time of stress when hungry and desperate men were prepared to defy the beliefs of their forefathers and pillage the deep-hidden tombs of their god-kings. The transcribed report is obviously a smoothed-over version of what the robber actually said. But no doubt the fluency and accuracy of his own account owed something to the lash which was applied regularly to the soles of his feet.

Tomb robbery was a risky trade, made even more dangerous because it outraged Egyptian religious ideals. But it also served an important economic function, as the Egyptologist John Wilson has suggested. The thieves restored to circulation an immense amount of silver and gold which had been stored away for the dead and thus withdrawn from the national economy. With the ending of the Bronze Age, Egypt had become poorer. It could no longer profit by mining the copper of the Sinai peninsula and manufacturing bronze for

A stone carver prepares a coffin.

an eager foreign market. Now it had to import iron itself for tools and weapons; and the fall of the Hittite empire, and the resultant breakdown in communications kept iron very expensive. As a result, grain prices rose and the government was unable to provide rations for the workmen who laboured on the tombs in the necropolis at Thebes. Some of them went on strike for their pay – the first recorded example of a labour dispute. Others chose a more direct and more effective method for getting the money they needed. They tunnelled into the tombs and plundered them.

Unlike the austere, unadorned galleries within the pyramids, the corridors of the later tombs were covered with painted reliefs depicting the progress of the dead pharaoh in the sun god's boat as it passed through the twelve caverns of the Underworld – the subterranean Nile upon which Amen-Re journeyed during the hours of night. Above and below these scenes are columns of hieroglyphic texts which recite spells from the Book of Him Who Is in the Underworld, in which the pharaoh is interrogated by the good and evil spirits he will meet during his subterranean journey.

In the Book of the Dead, another compilation of religious formulas, the primitive charms and spells of the Pyramid Texts that had served pharaohs of the early dynasties, were modified and expanded to fit the needs of persons of lesser rank. Such popular tomb magic probably meant as little to the average Egyptian as it does to us, but with the 'democratization' of the Osiris cult, it was intended to guide the departed spirit of every man through the realm of the gods. After winning an infernal game of questions and answers (he could hardly fail to win since he was provided with the correct answers), the dead man appeared before Osiris, judge of souls. The depictions of this scene, which often illuminate the papyrus rolls, usually include a pair of balances with the soul in one pan and the feather of *maat* in the other.

In the New Kingdom, as in former times, the Egyptian love of life still predominated. On the walls of the tombs of the nobles, cut out of the rock of the eastward-facing cliffs

With the deceased and his wife looking on, the funeral god Anubis weighs the heart of the scribe Ani, in an illustration from a papyrus Book of the Dead found in a New Kingdom tomb. The ceremony took place before the throne of Osiris, in the Hall of Double Justice, while a fierce hybrid monster called the Devourer waited near by, ready to consume the dead man's heart if it failed to balance with a feather (symbolizing truth) placed on the other scale-pan. Such illustrations invariably showed the scales in equilibrium as a token of favourable judgement. After the ibis-headed god Thoth recorded the results and Osiris pronounced his judgement, the deceased enjoyed eternal happiness.

Tomb paintings and monumental reliefs allowed artists little freedom to experiment. But on *ostraca* – potsherds or flakes of limestone – they were able to depict such things as this acrobatic dancer and a gazelle challenging a lion at draughts, in a frieze of animals.

at Thebes, we can recognize most of the subjects with which we have become familiar in the mastabas of the Old Kingdom – hunting, fishing, and party-giving. If anything they are less inhibited, as in one tomb that pictures a servant holding a bowl before a woman who has been overcome by her potations. Yet there was the other side to this picture.

> (One) generation passes away
> And others remain (in its place) . . .
> The gods that were aforetime
> Rest in their pyramids;
> Nobles and glorified likewise,
> Are buried in their pyramids.
> They that built houses,
> Their places are no more;
> What has been done with them?
> I have heard the sayings of Imhotep and Djedefhor,
> With whose words men still speak so much,
> What are their places?
> Their walls have crumbled,
> Their places are no more,
> As if they had never been.
> None cometh from thence
> That he might tell their circumstances,
> That he might tell their needs,
> And content our heart
> Until we have reached the place
> Whither they have gone. . . .

When the guests sat at their tables, heavy with wine, sated with

Eighteenth Dynasty tomb painting. In the partly destroyed upper register are the guests at a banquet, two married couples who sit arm-in-arm, waited upon by a servant girl. Below them, musicians wearing cones of pomade to perfume their elaborate wigs clap hands and sing.

music and the antics of dancing girls, an old blind man would pluck the strings of his harp and in his high voice sing an ancient song steeped in pessimism.

All the pharaohs of the New Kingdom from the beginning of the Eighteenth Dynasty to the end of the Twentieth were buried in the Valley of the Kings. Each was accompanied by such richness – in furniture, jewellery, arms, clothing, and personal adornment – as to make it certain that during those brief centuries this short and lonely valley contained a greater quantity of sheer wealth – in golden treasures and other works of art – than any place on the earth's surface. Of all these tombs only one survived almost intact, and that merely the

Another Eighteenth Dynasty tomb painting, showing female musicians entertaining guests at a banquet. They are playing a lute, a harp and a double flute; above them supplies for the feast include bunches of grapes and a garlanded wine-jug.

small, cramped sepulchre of a minor king, Tutankhamen. The fact that it kept its secrets down to the twentieth century is due to several factors. Tutankhamen, a boy-king who died at about eighteen years of age, reigned briefly at the end of the Eighteenth Dynasty, very shortly after the Akhenaten interlude; he was related to, and had been brought up at the court of, Akhenaten; and although he himself returned to orthodoxy, as his name indicates, his memory may have suffered from association with the heretic. It so happened that when the tomb of one of the later pharaohs was tunnelled into the hillside above Tutankhamen's tomb, the chippings from these operations hid the entrance to the young king's much more modest sepulchre.

So that, whereas even as far back as Roman times many of the tombs in the Royal Valley had become empty show-places for curious visitors, that of Tutankhamen escaped detection by the tomb robbers. More than a hundred generations had walked past that obscure grave, yet not one man in all that long time realized that so very near in the hillside lay treasures which, when discovered in 1922, would astound the world. The king's body was enclosed in a coffin of solid gold, so heavy that it required four men to lift it. This coffin nested within two outer coffins of wood, richly ornamented with gold, carnelian, and lapis; and these in turn were surrounded by a nest of timber shrines, plated with sheet gold, all richly worked and inscribed.

The objects found in the adjoining chambers now fill several of the principal galleries in the Egyptian Museum in Cairo. They range from the king's chariots and hunting gear down to the tiniest and most exquisitely made jewellery. There are the pharaoh's couches, chairs, and beds; chests containing his clothing, ebony and ivory caskets filled with weapons, toilet articles, and toys, including a game played with movable pieces, rather like chequers. There were statues covered with gold, vases, and other palace ornaments of translucent alabaster; rings, pectorals inlaid with semi-precious stones, and,

A blind musician plays the harp. In showing one arm realistically placed behind the harp, the sculptor has departed from one of the classic conventions of Egyptian art.

His solid gold inner coffin shows Tutankhamen holding the symbols of royal authority – a crook and a flail.

Lion decorating a funerary couch of Tutankhamen.

on the head of the body, a portrait mask of solid gold. All this treasure, the property of a minor pharaoh, was crammed into four small chambers cut like the others from the rock – one of the smallest royal tombs ever found. One can only speculate on the treasure that once filled the chambers of such great kings as Tuthmosis III, Sethi I, and Ramesses II and III.

By another miracle the bodies of these and other of the mightiest New Kingdom pharaohs were found in 1881, hidden in a forgotten tomb shaft on the eastern side of the Theban cliffs, where they had been stacked by the necropolis priests in a final, successful effort to protect the royal dead. The bodies had been rewrapped, in certain cases several times, but of the rich regalia with which they must have been surrounded in their original tombs hardly anything remained.

The bodies themselves lay undisturbed for three thousand years, so that today privileged visitors to the museum in Cairo can look into the faces of monarchs who once 'held the world in awe'. Sekenenre is there, still showing the wounds caused by the clubs and daggers of his enemies; so is Tuthmosis III, with

Because Egyptian convention required that Pharaoh be shown as an invincible conqueror, the peaceable young King Tutankhamen was depicted as a warrior, his plumed horses mercilessly trampling the bodies of Nubian enemies.

the intelligent face recognizable from his statues; the powerful, heavy-jawed face of the conqueror Sethi I; and the emaciated features of Ramesses II, who reigned for more than sixty years, and raised such numerous and massive monuments that he passed into legend as the mightiest of pharaohs.

None of the kings who followed even approached the power

and magnificence of these New Kingdom pharaohs, though, with interruptions, native Egyptian dynasties continued to reign down to the fourth century B.C. Even then, when one of Alexander's generals founded a new dynasty, these Greek-speaking, Greek-thinking conquerors became sufficiently Egyptianized to adopt pharaonic titles, religion, and customs. After three thousand years the valley dwellers' civilization was still tenacious, and even through this long, slow period of decline, the pharaohs occasionally attempted to reassert their ancient power.

They had strong rivals – the priests. Through the munificence or superstition of the pharaohs of the Eighteenth and Nineteenth Dynasties, the temple foundations gained a stranglehold on the economy of Egypt, and with it, on the government as well. The great temples had always been an important force in Egyptian life, but by the time of the Ramesside pharaohs they may have controlled as much as one tenth of the population. Eventually, the high priest of Amen ruled the southern half of the Nile Valley, from Thebes, while a merchant dynasty controlled the Delta region in the north. Even when the pharaoh did not bear the title of high priest, questions of state were often decided by a consultation with the oracles of the gods, with the priests interpreting the answers. It was a god who decided whether an erring office-holder should be brought to trial, or determined the allotment of a disputed inheritance; a god chose new government officials from a list submitted to his shrine. This reliance on oracles meant that in essence the priests shared sovereignty with the king. This was not the only symbol of the changes which occurred in the religion of Egypt during the Late Period. Egyptians had always been concerned with ceremonial observances; but now ritual became of fanatical importance, with punctilious attention paid to detail. In earlier ages, certain animals had been revered as manifestation of the gods; now they were worshipped themselves. Thousands of them were piously tended during their lives and carefully mummified upon their death. Extensive cemeteries were set aside specifically for the interment of sacred cats or crocodiles. The Greeks looked on these features of Egyptian religion with curiosity and awe; the Hebrews with scorn.

Apart from a few references to the *Habiru*, a name which may denote the Hebrew tribes, Egyptian chronicles rarely mention the Jews, and no one can state definitely under which pharaoh Moses lived. The biblical account of the captivity in Egypt records that the children of Israel 'built for Pharaoh treasure cities, Pithom and Raamses'. Raamses was probably the city of Tanis in the Delta, renamed after Ramesses II when he established his capital there. It may have been Ramesses who was the pharaoh during the Exodus, which many scholars date to the thirteenth century B.C. In any case it is likely that the Jews left Egypt before the time of his successor, Merneptah; on a memorial stele boasting of his conquests, that ruler announces, rather prematurely, 'Israel is laid waste, his seed is not.'

We are on much more firm ground when about three hundred years later the Old Testament mentions 'Shishak, King of Egypt', to whom Jeroboam fled 'and was in Egypt unto the death of Solomon'. This king was undoubtedly Sheshonq, first king of the Twenty-second Dynasty who invaded Palestine and Judea in the fifth year of his reign (945 B.C.). According to the Book of Kings, Shishak

> came up against Jerusalem. And he took away the treasures of the house of the Lord, and the treasures of the king's house; he even took away all: and he took away all the shields of gold which Solomon had made. . . .

The tomb of one of this king's successors, also named Sheshonq, was discovered as recently as 1940 by Professor Montet at the Delta city of Tanis, almost certainly the Old Testament Zoan, and the capital of Egypt at this period. He and the other pharaohs of the Twenty-first and Twenty-second Dynasties were Libyans. Although Thebes was still the focus of religious power, dominated by priest-kings who did not recognize the authority, such as it was, of the northern rulers, Tanis had become a great capital. One day, we can hope, some lucky excavator at Tanis may recover the treasures which Sheshonq took from Solomon's temples.

This was the first time in three hundred years that an Egyptian king had invaded Palestine; and it may have seemed, at the time, that the days of Egypt's imperial glory were about to return. But soon other powers – the Assyrians, Babylonians, and later the Persians – took the place that the kings of Egypt's imperial age had once occupied. Egypt relied increasingly on foreign troops, and except for one last revival never again commanded the resources and the militant patriotism of a united realm. Moreover she was outclassed in weapons and military tactics.

In the Old Testament the Assyrian envoys sneer at the Judean king for relying on the king of Egypt – 'this broken reed' – as an ally. Between 715 and 300 B.C. Egypt was occupied for shorter or longer periods by various foreign conquerors: by the Kushites, the Assyrians, the Persians, and the Macedonians. The Kushites established a brief dynasty, the Persians ruled from the time of Cambyses (525 B.C.) down to that of Darius II (424–404 B.C.), son of Xerxes. Yet between the Twenty-fifth (Kushite) and the Twenty-seventh (Persian) Dynasties Egypt knew an Indian summer under the Saites – native Egyptian kings who came from Sais, and governed the land for more than a century during which Egyptians assiduously imitated the art and literature of the Old Kingdom in an attempt to revive the glories that had so long been a part of the past.

It was during this period that the Greeks began to enter Egypt, at first as mercenaries, then as traders and merchants. They found the three-thousand-year-old civilization still in being, its political power waning but its ancient culture remarkably enduring. The Greeks marvelled at it, and in the writings of Herodotus we can feel the wonder and respect that these questing, intelligent, curious people felt when confronted by the Egyptian colossus. Although he has been dubbed 'the father of lies', Herodotus was accurate in many of his conclusions. Like a conscientious modern journalist he listened to and reported what he was told, without necessarily believing it, and like a modern journalist he sometimes repeated hearsay with tongue-in-cheek. Much of the information that he gained from the Egyptian priests has since been proved to be true; and at least he had the enviable opportunity of seeing Egyptian civilization still in being, magnificently surviving the misfortunes of defeat and foreign occupation.

A little over a century after Herodotus' visit the Ptolemies came to Egypt and founded its last dynasty. Sophisticated Hellenes though they were, the Ptolemies too succumbed to the lure of this all but timeless civilization – the longest-lived of all ancient cultures. They became pharaohs, and are represented in sculpture very much as were their predecessors who had ruled Egypt thirty centuries earlier. And when Cleopatra, last of the Ptolemies and the last native ruler of ancient Egypt, died, she did so with a gesture which is dramatically appropriate to her nature. For the 'asp' that Shakespeare tells of the slave bringing into Cleopatra's presence in a basket was the royal cobra – the symbol that Egyptian pharaohs had worn on their crowns since the beginnings of dynastic history. Cleopatra was killed by one of the most ancient deities of Egypt – the goddess Wadjet, guardian of Buto, in the Delta where Egyptian civilization budded and flowered so many long centuries before.

Colossi of Amenhotep III.

2 The Land Between the Rivers

1 · Sumer, Dawn of Civilization

Several of the world's earliest civilizations developed in the crescent-shaped area of south-western Asia that stretches from Palestine on the Mediterranean, curving around northern Arabia, to the Persian Gulf in the east. From time immemorial mountaineers from the northern uplands and nomads from the deserts to the south struggled for possession of these lands. Most of the eastern half of the crescent, the land that slopes down in grassy steppes from the mountains of Armenia and follows the Tigris and Euphrates rivers to their outlet in the Gulf, falls within the territory of modern Iraq.

The visitor to Iraq will look in vain for anything comparable to the natural and man-made wonders to be found in Egypt. Few awesome ruins remain to recall the mighty civilizations which flourished there. The stony uplands of the north give way to brown plains of almost unbearable flatness which extend from horizon to horizon. From the air, this desolate landscape looks like sand, but on landing, say, at Baghdad, the visitor will find that it is in fact dried alluvial mud brought down by the two great rivers, the Tigris and Euphrates, the sole sources of Iraq's fertility. As they flow across the broad flatlands on their way to the Persian Gulf, these twin arteries

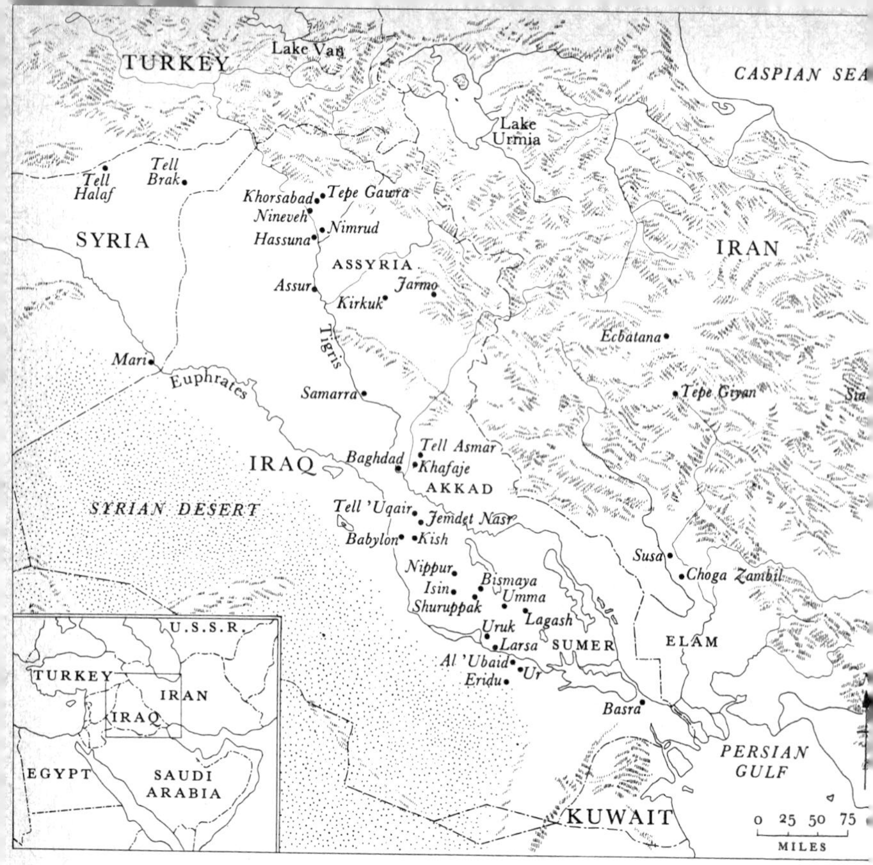

Sumer and Akkad.

meander erratically, often changing their course. They are uncontrolled by natural barriers. No cliffs hem them in, and the only constraints put upon them are those erected by men – the great embankments or levees that throw long shadows at sunrise and sunset. In the southern valley one can trace a network of straight lines that is hardly visible at ground level but can be seen from the air, marking the pattern of long-vanished irrigation canals.

Apart from Islamic cities such as Baghdad, and clusters of black Bedouin tents, one sees few signs of human habitation. Here and there a modern pipeline, a dam, and a glinting reservoir; the rest appears to be wasteland. South of Baghdad, near Basra, the rivers filter through a broad marshland and join to form a single large stream that shortly empties into the Gulf. From the air, one can see a waste of muddy water, patterned with symmetrical 'stars' which one later discovers are the tops of half-submerged palm trees. The gleaming wet banks of brown leviathans occasionally rear out of the water, mudbanks on which may be discerned the moving figures of men and their cattle, and the green patches which are their crops.

This drab valley that stretches from the Gulf to the Armenian mountains in the north is the Land Between the Rivers – Mesopotamia, as the ancient Greeks called it. In and about this valley, long before the classic age of Greece, centred the great empires of Assyria and Babylonia. And here, more than two millenniums still earlier, the Sumerians developed a remarkable civilization which, antedating even that of Egypt, was the earliest known on earth.

Some four thousand years ago, the Sumerians set down in writing their conception of how their river-bound world was created, recording a myth that was ancient even at that time. The story is echoed in the first chapter of Genesis, for the Hebrew writers almost certainly derived their idea of creation, like the Garden of Eden, the tale of the Deluge, and other traditional stories in the Old Testament, from the Land Between the Rivers.

> And God said, let there be a firmament in the midst of the waters, and let it divide the waters from the waters. And God made the firmament, and divided the waters which were under the firmament from the waters which were above the firmament: and it was so. . . . And God said, let the waters under the heaven be gathered together unto one place, and let dry land appear: and it was so.

If one thinks of the earth as a spinning globe, this biblical interpretation of creation is not easy to reconcile with known facts, except in a poetic sense. But if for *firmament* one thinks simply of the lower valley of the Tigris-Euphrates, a land of wide-spreading flood, marshes, mudbanks, and clouds, it does make sense. Gods and goddesses are the chief participants in the story, because these early peoples saw what we call natural phenomena as the acts of their deities or the manifestations of the gods themselves.

To the people of that valley, the fresh-water flood was Apsu, and the salt-water sea in the distance with which Apsu mingled in the primordial chaos, was Tiamat. The mingling of the two resulted in a deposit of silt brought down by the rivers, which gave birth to Enki, the god of earth, and Anu, god of heaven. Then Enlil, god of the air and the most important deity in the Sumerian pantheon, separated the heaven and earth which had been born of the waters, the way the God of Hebrews divided the waters to make dry land appear. It was Enlil too who taught the Sumerians agriculture and gave them tools with which to build. Archaeology cannot corroborate the myth of Enlil's teaching, but it can follow the record of how the people of Mesopotamia learned to farm and build, and how the river valley slowly developed a complex urban civilization.

By 7000 B.C. the agricultural revolution had begun on the fringes of these regions; man had already begun to gather cereal crops, thus partly freeing himself from the necessity of hunting game for his food. In widely separated sites, among the mountains of Iran and in the upper Tigris Valley of Iraq and south-eastern Turkey, archaeologists have discovered the settlements of these early farmers. There is one at Qalat Jarmo, in the grassy uplands of northern Iraq, close to the modern city of Kirkuk.

From the air, the site looks something like a circular mudpie from which a substantial segment has been eaten away by a stream. On the very edge of this eroded portion, one sees a series of mathematically spaced test pits in which archaeologists have dug down through twenty-three feet of occupational debris to establish their evidence. From about 7000 B.C., Jarmo was occupied by a succession of primitive agricultural communities, whose farmers used flint-bladed sickles to reap their grain; they domesticated goats, and perhaps dogs as well. They built straight-sided dwellings of bricks made of pressed mud. On the lower, that is earlier, levels of the site, the excavators found stone vessels. On higher and therefore later levels of occupation, coarse pottery appeared, and figurines of animals made of baked clay.

Jarmo is one of the most ancient settlements in Mesopotamia. Comparable sites that have been discovered by archaeologists have been assigned various dates ranging from 5500 to 4000 B.C., although precise dating is impossible. All were the settlements of primitive hunter-farmers who gradually moved down into the Tigris-Euphrates Valley seeking more desirable land. There is no historical record of these movements, except obliquely in legend, but a scientific examination of the stratigraphy of these sites, which has been undertaken in the course of many seasons, reveals a fascinating story.

At Hassuna in northern Iraq, it is possible to trace the development of the town from the time when man first camped there to the days when he had begun to make substantial buildings. Here in the bottom layer next to the virgin soil, the excavators found a camp site strewn with tools of stone and bone, crude pottery containers, and clay pellets for use in slings; but there was no trace of any dwelling. Here, perhaps, a group of nomads had moved down from the mountains, probably in spring, and camped on the fertile grasslands at the junction of two streams. They were attracted, no doubt, by the abundance of game and fish, and the possibility of reaping a crop of wild barley before the winter storms forced them to move on. Later, when they returned, they found that the trees were again bearing fruit, and there was more wild barley. In time the idea would occur to someone that they might settle here, and build some form of protection against winter conditions.

And this is evidently what happened. In the next stage, the nomads had learned to sow the crops which they had seen growing there; later still, mud huts appear and better pottery, until at last, near the top of the mound, were the remains of a complete agricultural community, hardly differing from that of the neighbouring village of Hassuna in the twentieth century. There is no evidence to show when cattle, sheep, and pigs were domesticated, but bones of a pig were found in an early level at the site. At about 4000 B.C., prehistoric Hassuna seems to have been abandoned.

To the imaginative mind, such a story, based purely on layers of pottery fragments, mud-brick foundations, and primitive tools, is as stirring as the tale of the Tower of Babel, for here, to borrow Gordon Childe's phrase, is 'man in the making'. Let there be no doubt that the descendants of such people built the great Sumerian cities with their towering ziggurats, invented writing, and developed mathematics and astronomy, and created a culture that survived down to the time of the classical Greeks. There were many Hassunas; again and again in the mountains north and east of Mesopotamia, archaeologists have found the remains of similar communities, and through their characteristic artifacts, especially pottery, have been able to trace the progress of their culture into the valley of the twin rivers.

It is not easy for the layman to appreciate just how important pottery is to the archaeologist, and why he rates bits of earthenware so highly. Some half century ago, an Oxford scholar appraised its value to the researcher.

> For 'tis not verse and 'tis not prose
> But earthenware alone
> It is that ultimately shows
> What men have thought and done.

It is fairly true to say that the history of the human species as revealed by archaeology alone, without benefit of written records, is little more than a history of technology and artifacts; when he finds no written records, all the archaeologist can hope to do at a given site is to study the building foundations and objects found at various levels. Pottery is the most common

of these artifacts, and part of its value lies in the fact that it provides a trade mark or 'brand name' by which we can follow the development of a particular culture and observe how it spreads.

If a characteristic form of storage jar originally found at Site A turns up at Sites B, C, and D in a later context, it is reasonable to assume that the people or the culture represented by type A had spread to these other regions, either through physical conquest or the peaceful superimposition of one culture upon another. Similarly, minor variations among pottery styles are significant, for in Mesopotamia as elsewhere the beginnings and development of a civilization often can be traced only by observing the changes in its pottery, and in its tools and weapons – objects that are often small, unromantic, and of little beauty. Yet rightly interpreted, they are no less

In this frieze, which shows one aspect of farming, priests are seen at work on the sacred dairy farm of Ninhursaga, the Sumerian mother goddess. At the right they milk the cows (from behind) while muzzled calves look on. To the left, past a cow barn made of reeds, one priest pours the milk through a funnel or strained held by a seated companion; two others on either side hold large jars, in which they may be preparing butter. The figures were carved from shell and white limestone and inlaid in shale between raised borders of copper. Found at al'Ubaid, near Ur, the frieze dates from early in the third millennium B.C.

significant than the great pyramids, the Theban tombs, and the other enormous and impressive monuments of Egypt.

Neolithic settlements like Hassuna were succeeded by those of a people called the Tell Halaf folk, who established themselves for many centuries in the hill country and plains of northern Mesopotamia. Later, to their south, a new wave of migrants entered the river valley from the highlands of Iran. These, the al 'Ubaid people, were farmers and stockbreeders, skilled in many crafts. They used implements of stone and flint, and produced greenish pots of varying shapes, with designs in black paint.

'Gallant heroes lived before Agamemnon, not a few; but on all alike, unwept and unknown, eternal night lies heavy because they lack a sacred poet,' Horace said, and there must have been more than one of such forgotten geniuses who led mankind on its upward path, and whose bones lie scattered among the fragmented pottery of these Stone and Bronze Age villages. The Sargons, the Gudeas, and the Hammurabis, the great leaders of later times, were fortunate in being born after the invention of writing, and at a time when technological advances had enabled them to leave permanent memorials. The leaders who first induced their followers to settle in one place instead of wandering, and who later led them to move to more advantageous situations, against the force of tradition, have left no record. But they must have existed, if only for the reason that in historical times we know that important advances are normally initiated by such gifted and forceful individuals, and do not ordinarily arise by accident or by the drift of circumstances alone.

Who was it, for instance, who inspired the events recorded in the eleventh chapter of the Book of Genesis?

> And it came to pass, as they journeyed from the east, that they found a plain in the land of Shinar; and they dwelt there. And they said to one another, 'Go to, let us make brick and burn them thoroughly.' And they had brick for stone, and slime had they for mortar. And they said, 'Go to, let us build a city, and a tower, whose top may reach unto heaven; and let us make a name, lest we be scattered abroad upon the face of the whole earth.'

Archaeology has revealed that this is indeed what happened,

though not suddenly as in the biblical story that tells of the Tower of Babel, but over a long period of time. Some of the early immigrants to southern Mesopotamia (Sumer, the land of Shinar) probably did come from the east. They found a fertile land, but one without stone, so they learned to make bricks from the river mud, and eventually to burn them thoroughly in kilns. And they evolved the ziggurat, or temple tower, perhaps to remind them and their gods of the mountainous lands from which they had come.

At the site of the ancient city of Eridu excavators have found at a number of early levels remains of large temples which undoubtedly date from the al 'Ubaid period, that is, from about 4000 to 3500 B.C. But it was the succeeding Uruk period (3800–3200 B.C.) that witnessed an extensive development of monumental architecture and the evolution of the first real cities. For instance, at Uruk itself there was a large temple with its shrine built on a raised platform, a forerunner of the ziggurats or giant, many-tiered towers central to most later Mesopotamian cities. The sacred buildings in Uruk were colourfully decorated with mosaic patterns made up of clay cones dipped in pigment and decoratively arranged. At 'Uqair, another site of this period, there were wall paintings representing processions of human and animal figures. This richness and exuberance of decoration, no less than the scale of the buildings mentioned, provides impressive testimony to the level of accomplishment reached in the land of Sumer as early as the fourth millennium B.C.

But the Uruk people may be given credit for an even more important innovation, the development of writing. It is at this time that we find the first primitive pictographs from which the later cuneiform writing system evolved in a manner that can be accurately traced.

Just how writing originated we cannot be sure, but it was certainly for utilitarian reasons, through a need for keeping records. Among the early nomadic peoples trade and commerce were no more highly organized than they are in primitive African or South American tribes today. Permanent records were not needed; human memory was sufficient. But once human beings began to be organized in large and complex

Clay tablet with pre-cuneiform pictographs; the small circles represent numbers.

social groups, with varying interdependent relationships, and were faced with the problems of accumulating, storing, and distributing surplus wealth, the need for a more permanent and accurate system of recording became urgent.

The earliest intelligible examples of writing are inventories. They are lists of objects: so many head of cattle, so many jars of oil, so many captives. From early times – long before he had evolved an architecture or a written language, as we can see from examples of palaeolithic art in the caves of south-western Europe and of Africa – man has enjoyed exercising his skill in drawing the world about him. Hence it is natural that most of the earliest writing symbols were pictures: a rudimentary cow's head, a man or a woman, a wine jar, a sword or a shield, the disk of the sun or moon.

Originally these would be used as a reminder, for example, that A had agreed to exchange with B so many cows for so many jars of oil, the barter to be completed within so many months. A series of crude pictures of cows, oil jars, and moons (each representing a month) would suffice to record the bargain. Later this system would be elaborated more and more until a time came when the pictographs gave way to a series of conventional signs, which were easier to write and which were no longer representations of objects, but of the sounds of human speech. Obviously numeration was also evolved, a series of dots or strokes representing numbers. Thus writing was born, with all its vast potential for recording not merely commercial transactions but the achievements of rulers, hymns and invocations to the gods, the practical knowledge that grew along with man's gradual mastery of his environment, the wisdom of thinkers and philosophers, and the imaginative flights of story-tellers and poets.

This new means of communications appears to have evolved first in Mesopotamia. As we have seen, the idea may well have inspired the predynastic Egyptians to develop their own writing system. There is, however, a basic difference between Sumerian and Egyptian writing, which is almost certainly due to the type of writing materials that were available in the two lands. In Egypt, where stone was abundant, the pictorial form of writing survived for monumental inscriptions down to the time of Roman rule, although when writing on papyrus the scribes used a flowing, cursive form called the hieratic. In Sumer, though the system undoubtedly began as a series of pictographs, these were rapidly modified until writing became

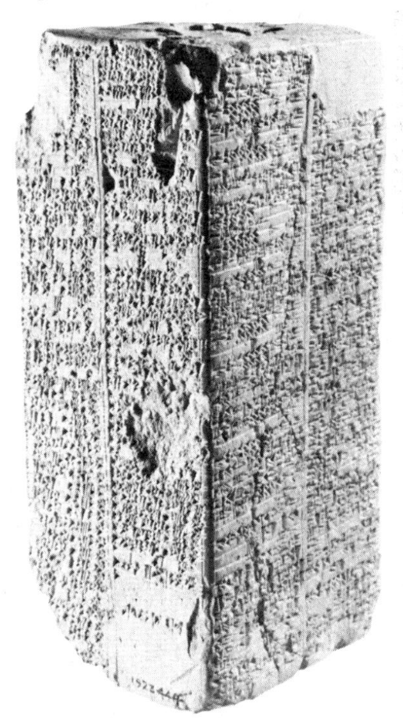

The cuneiform texts on this prism comprise the Sumerian King List, which chronicles the passage of 'the kingship' from one city of Sumer to another, from the time it was 'lowered from heaven' till about 2000 B.C.

merely a series of little wedge-shaped marks (hence *cuneiform* – 'wedge-shaped'). The Sumerians wrote on the same abundantly available material they used for their buildings – mud. It is difficult to write pictographs on wet clay, but wedges are easy to make. Nearly all Mesopotamian writings are on clay tablets, usually about the size of a postal card, convenient to work, to handle, and to store. Although fragile and easily crushed, thousands of them have survived and more turn up continually on the sites of ancient Mesopotamian cities. And it is from these precious writings, far more than from the once-mighty ziggurats, temples, and palaces, that we are able to trace the history of each of the successive Mesopotamian civilizations.

For it is important to remember that in Mesopotamia we are dealing not with one but with several 'lost worlds'. Egypt's natural barriers protected the Nile world against unwelcome outside influence and intrusion. Unprotected by such barriers, the fertile plains and valleys of Mesopotamia attracted migrants and invaders, settlers and conquerors, who invested the land in successive waves over the course of a long time. In spite of the frequent changes that resulted, the basic pattern of civilization established by the early Sumerians remained fairly constant. The racial and linguistic affinities of the Sumerians – 'the black-headed people', as they called themselves – are unknown. Their language was neither Indo-European nor Semitic. But the cuneiform script they evolved was taken over by the Akkadians, the Babylonians, the Assyrians, and other peoples who later ruled in Mesopotamia, and with it were perpetuated many of the myths and legends, the proverbs and poems, the medical and mathematical lore that made up the abundant literature of the Sumerians, and with this their basic culture.

Before 2500 B.C. the land of Sumer was occupied by a number of independent city-states. There was no single, centralized political authority as there was in Egypt. The earliest city-states were primitive democracies, ruled by assembles of all adult men (except slaves). Only in time of crisis did the assembly elect a king and hand over absolute power to him for the duration of the emergency. But as relations among the cities became more complex and threatening, kingship became permanent rather than temporary. The kings of these early centres did not claim divine status for themselves, as Egyptians and later Mesopotamian rulers did; in fact, the Sumerian word for king can also be translated simply as 'great man'. Each of these urban communities owed allegiance primarily to a local deity and each of them was surrounded by, and largely dependent upon, an extensive agricultural hinterland.

These city-states represented a new stage in social organization. They arose because circumstances in southern Mesopotamia encouraged the organized, cooperative efforts of the community. Here the land was made abundantly fertile by the river-borne mud. But before this fertility could be effectively exploited, the rivers had to be controlled, and the large-scale system of irrigation that was developed to meet this need involved a complex social organization. With an elaborate system of canals that throughout the dry summer months conserved the water brought down by the winter floods, a land which earlier sustained no more than a handful of villages could now support a prolific population. And with the surplus of produce that resulted, some part of the population was freed from devoting all of its time and energies to the unremitting task of providing food. Some men were able to function as specialists – priests, carpenters, metalworkers, sculptors, and so forth. Foremost among these were the priests and rulers, men who governed and protected the land, who understood and could interpret the mysterious, terrifying phenomena of sun, rain, flood, tempest, which ultimately controlled men's lives – the forces which would bring abundance or famine, wealth or poverty, which produced fertility or sterility in men, cattle, or crops. These were the wise men who understood how the earth began, and how the powers kept it in equilibrium.

Below this higher intellectual class, but allied with it, were the administrators and civil servants, the scribes who had learned the secret of writing and who kept records of crop yields, flood levels, years of plenty or of dearth, annual returns from taxation, the movement of the stars, and the achievements of their great men. Below them were other classes: the architects and builders who planned and erected palaces and temples; the artisans who understood the craft of working clay, stone, and in time, metal; the carpenters, boatmen, jewellers; the spinners and weavers, who were usually slaves. There was also a very important class of traders and merchants who, among other things, brought in sorely needed commodities from the world outside the valley.

There were many Sumerian cities bordering the Tigris and Euphrates: Eridu, Khafaje, Lagash, Shuruppak, Uruk (which the Bible calls Erech), the great ceremonial centre of Nippur, and Ur, the city where, according to tradition, Abraham the patriarch was born. Though they were scattered over a wide area, were varied in size, and owed allegiance to separate gods, their basic character was similar. They rose from a level plain, on or near a river. Their structures were almost entirely of mud bricks, but with this modest building material they achieved monumental effects. Surrounding each city there was probably a defensive wall, as for example at Uruk. At Khafaje there was a series of interior walls, graduated in height, surrounding the temple at the centre of the city; within these were rows of workmen's houses and shops, stores and warehouses. If the city was on a river, wharves were provided for vessels.

Dominating the city and the fertile fields, vineyards, orchards and pastures that surrounded it, rose the temple of the chief deity, usually placed upon a high artificial mound. As early as the fourth millennium B.C. one temple complex at Uruk covered an area of almost half a million square feet, its shrine rising from a platform that was forty feet high. Later these sacred temple towers, or ziggurats (the Mesopotamian word means 'to be high' or 'pointed') occasionally achieved phenomenal height and bulk. Their construction must have consumed millions of man-hours of labour. They have been compared with the pyramids of Egypt, but they were of course not tombs. They served quite a different purpose. Each of these structures was in effect an artificial mountain raised by gigantic efforts of the community to bridge the gap between man and god. A temple was placed at the top of the tower to serve as a chamber of welcome for the god descending from heaven. At the ground level another shrine was usually provided for the accommodation of the deity during his stay on earth. Processional stairways linked the two, inevitably bringing to mind Jacob's vision of the 'ladder' that reached to heaven, on which he saw 'the angels of God ascending and descending'.

We might be tempted to compare this temple complex with a cathedral, or perhaps a great monastery; but these would be false analogies. In fact there is no modern equivalent. For the god or goddess of the city was the core of its existence; the activity of the community was primarily devoted to the interests of the temple. Religion was not something which could be separated from daily life. Even the use of the word *religion* to describe Sumerian belief conveys the wrong impression, because today we stress religion's association with a system of ethics and morality. In ancient Sumer, as in other early societies, the concept of religion included more immediate and practical meanings as well.

Gods and demons controlled every aspect of life; the natural

This gypsum figure stood at a temple altar in Nippur about 2700 B.C. as a woman's constant suppliant before her goddess. Its gold mask was once attached to a wooden head.

Figurines from the Square Temple at Tell Asmar. Most represent worshippers, but the two tallest, with their enormous eyes, may be a god and goddess, and the clean-shaven man in front of them is a priest.

forces of wind, rain, flood, and sun, and the gods and goddesses which personified them, either permitted men to live or destroyed them. These deities required constant propitiation, and it would have been calamitous to neglect or vary the elaborate rituals which appeased them. According to legend, the Sumerians had been created to live as serfs on the estates of the gods, to 'be burdened with the toil of the gods thet they may freely breathe'. And the Sumerians found their divine masters as capricious as human ones.

Although they were occasionally compassionate, the gods could be angry, vengeful, and selfish. Like human beings, they appreciated good food and wine, fine clothing, and other delights of mortal civilization. Like human beings, they married and had children, and sometimes quarrelled among themselves. They were also conscious of status; it would not have done, for instance, for the deity of Uruk to possess a temple inferior to that of the god who controlled Eridu.

To the Sumerians of all social classes, these deities were as real as the king and his hierarchy of priests, who administered the estates of the gods. The farmer at work in the barley fields, straightening to ease his back, would see rising above the waving grain the temple complex, dedicated to the god whose needs he supplied and whose priests in turn supplied him with seed, tools, and cattle for ploughing, and food and clothing for himself and his family. The same was true higher up the social scale: the scribes who kept accounts of crop yields and stores; the privileged priests who brought the god his offerings of food, and washed his sacred image and changed its clothing; the soldiers who fought the god's wars against neighbouring city-states; the merchants who exchanged wheat and barley for precious metals; the craftsmen who made beautiful objects of wood, stone, and ivory for the temples and palaces – all felt themselves to be the servants of the god.

Every Sumerian was equal before the gods. In the earliest period, all men had been assigned tasks to perform as divine service, and all were given rations from the temple storerooms, as well as allotments of land which they could farm for themselves. Eventually this system developed divisions of labour and class distinctions. The economy of the Sumerian temple community, that is, of the city-state, has been termed a system of theocratic socialism. Yet from an early date personal ownership of wealth was recognized and there remained ample opportunities for private enterprise. Imported luxuries, and luxuries of imported materials, that have been found in private tombs give but one indication that these opportunities for individual trade ventures were not neglected.

Perhaps the most extraordinary and moving example of the Sumerian spirit of collective devotion was found in the death pits of Ur, discovered by Leonard Woolley in 1923. Near the city walls Woolley came upon a cemetery that had been considerably plundered. Among its nearly two thousand graves were sixteen that clearly belonged to distinguished personages. They may have been kings and queens as Woolley thought, but we cannot be certain. The sepulchral chambers were of stone, which must have been brought from thirty miles away. Within each chamber lay a body, male or female, in full regalia of gold, silver, and semi-precious stones. Some had golden drinking cups beside them. These stone-built rooms lay at the bottom of deep pits which were approached by sloping ramps. Within the pits, and sometimes on the approach ramps, lay the bodies of scores of men, women, and animals. There were sixty-eight women in one pit, all of whom had been buried in red woollen robes, with head-dresses of gold or silver. Some of the women had musical instruments, such as lyres and harps made of wood and ornamented with gold, silver, shell, lapis lazuli, and red stone. They were probably court musicians. The wood of these instruments had decayed, but its impression remained in the soil, so that the archaeologists, by taking wax casts, were able to reconstruct the harps, replacing the rich gold and silver mountings so that they may now be seen in all their original beauty. These mounted decorations were most commonly fashioned in the form of an animals' head, that of a cow, or a magnificently bearded bull. In one case the complete figure of a stag is represented.

In another pit, Woolley found the remains of two wagons, with the bones of oxen and the bodies of their riders or drivers beside them. In a third pit lay soldiers in copper helmets, their spears at their sides.

The bodies were lying in orderly rows, giving the impression that these people had met a peaceful death or that the corpses had been tidied up afterwards. The little cups that lay beside them may have contained poison or a drug. It is possible that these servitors were alive when they entered the pits and, like the 'great ones' in the burial chambers, they were self-immolated. It seems not altogether unlikely that they went to their deaths calmly, without fuss. As they marched down into the pits they may even have been singing and the musicians playing.

After they became unconscious someone must indeed have entered the pits to tidy up the bodies before the earth was flung down on them; two of the harps lay *on top* of the corpses. Another poignant and significant detail is that half the court ladies had worn gold circlets in their hair; from the presence of certain oxides in the soil Woolley suspected that the rest had worn silver circlets, but he could not prove this. Then one day he found, near one of the bodies, a little metal disk, which on examination proved to be just such a silver circlet, tightly wound up in a coil. From this Woolley deduced that each girl had been so provided, but that whereas the majority had had time to put on their circlets, one girl – late for her own funeral – had left it coiled up in a pocket in her clothing which protected it from the corrosion that had destroyed the rest of the silver fillets.

What can one make of this? It is too facile to suggest that these victims had gone to their deaths joyously because they anticipated, like Christians or Moslems, a better world to come. A *better* world? Listen to a Sumerian description of the afterlife, where

> . . . the Dead shuffle
> Under their black plumage. . . . Where the food is clay
> And the drink ashes . . . whence there is no reprieve. . . .

Or this passage from another, later poem:

> When Inanna ascends from the nether world,
> Verily the dead hasten ahead of her.
> Inanna ascends from the nether world,
> The small demons like spear shafts,

The large demons like the spear shafts . . .
Walked at her side. . . .
They who accompanied Inanna,
Were beings who know not food, who know not water,
Who eat not sprinkled flour,
Who drink not libated water,
Who take away the wife from the loins of man,
Who take away the child from the . . . of the nursemaid.

Obviously the Sumerians did not view death and the hereafter with the confident hopes of the early Egyptians. Yet these well-fed, well-dressed Sumerian ladies and gentlemen of 4500 years ago, whose remains Woolley found in the death pits, apparently went to their graves calmly. If they had been driven into the pits and forced to kill themselves, would not there have been some signs of violence and terror?

There can be no certain answer to all this. It seems a likely possibility that the victims, without hope of future beatitude, allowed themselves to be sacrificed because they believed it to be a religious duty necessary for the safety of the city-state, whose well-being could be renewed only by the sacrifice of a king, or a mock king, and his retainers. The epic poem about Gilgamesh describes such a custom of sending retainers to accompany the dead king to his tomb. And it has parallels in numerous ancient societies. As late as the First Dynasty in Egypt the servants of a princess were slain upon her death and their bodies interred beside hers.

What the Ur tombs do clearly reveal is the wealth and beauty and fine craftsmanship which the 'great ones' of the period could command. The gold, silver, bronze, and semi-precious stones may have been imported, probably from Iran in exchange for Sumerian textiles, foodstuffs, tools, and weapons. The quality of the workmanship is highly sophisticated and reflects a long tradition of development. The fantastic head-dress of one of the sacrificed women, as absurdly delightful as a modern Paris hat; the upreared figure of a he-goat in gold and lapis, which has often been compared to the biblical 'ram caught in a thicket'; the splendid electrum helmet of another victim which reproduces a Sumerian style of male hair-do with chignon at the back; the beautifully wrought

Onager standing atop a rein ring, found in one of the royal tombs at Ur.

Head-dress found in a death pit of the Royal Cemetery. Probably worn over a large wig, it is crowned by a tall silver 'comb' decorated with inlaid flowers; beneath it are three beaded wreaths with gold pendants in the form of long willow leaves, beech leaves, and disks with lapis centres.

[Opposite] Sumerian figure of a goat and tree. Twenty inches high and made of gold foil, shell, and lapis over a wood core, it was found in the Royal Cemetery at Ur.

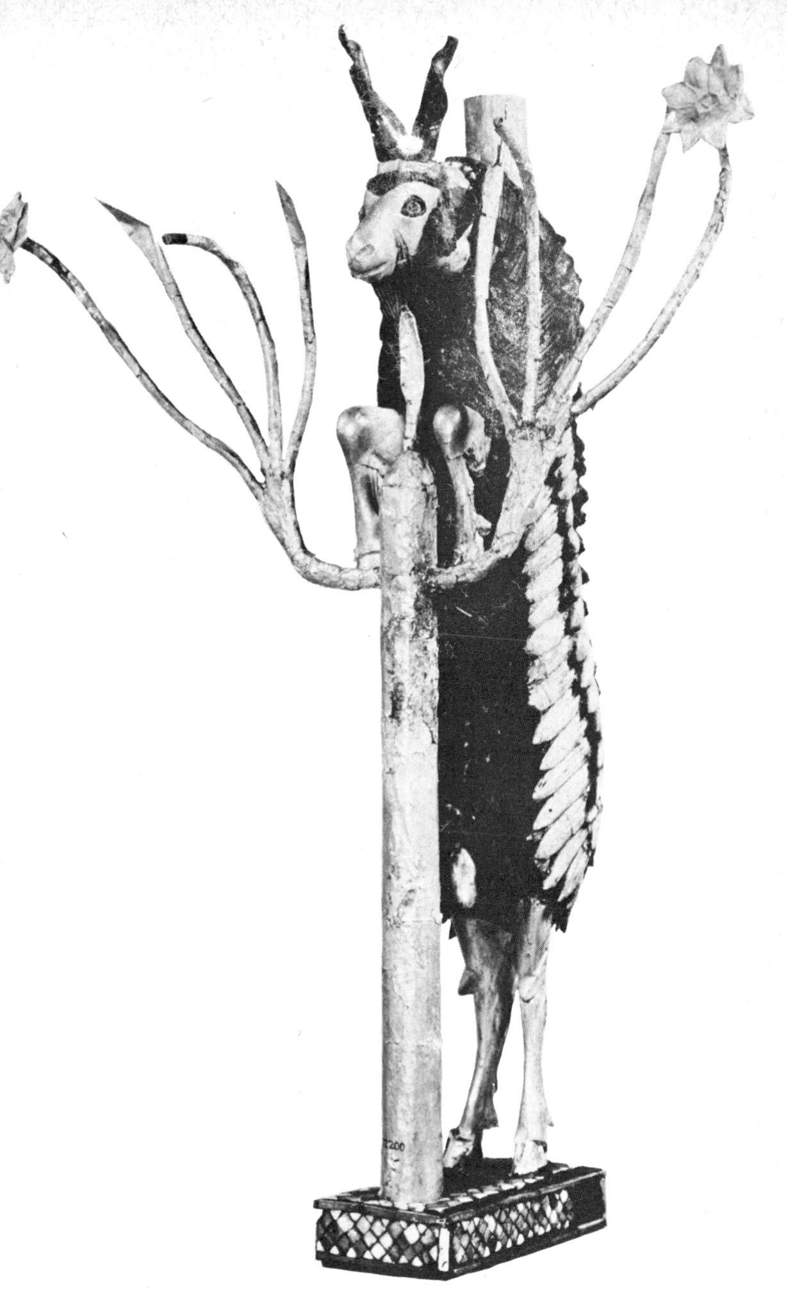

Helmet, from the Royal Cemetery at Ur, hammered from a single sheet of gold alloy. Laces through the holes round the edges held a padded lining. It is supposed, from a cylinder seal found in the same tomb, that the helmet belonged to a young man named Meskalam-dug who lived about 2500 B.C. He may have been a prince, for his grave, though not one of the so-called royal tombs, held uncommon riches.

golden drinking vessels – all these are comparable to the best Egyptian work of the same period.

The scenes depicted in lapis and inlaid shell on the sound boxes of the musical instruments and on other surfaces present fascinating and tantalizing images of this distant and often inscrutable world. On the famous 'Ur Standard' we see Sumerian infantry marching in step, spears ready, driving before them captured enemy prisoners. We see the king's chariot, drawn by wild asses (onagers), charging the enemy. These solid-wheeled chariots look clumsy compared with the graceful, spoked-wheeled vehicles of later times, but they were sturdy and no doubt powerful instruments of war at that time. On the reverse side of the 'Standard' are scenes of peace, perhaps a victory banquet, showing the king and his nobles

Victory was celebrated by a feast such as that shown on the 'Standard' from the Royal Cemetery at Ur. In the upper register the king sits facing his officers while, at the right, a female singer or dancer and a musician with a bull's head harp provide entertainment. The middle register shows bulls, rams, and fish being taken to the banquet table. At the bottom are teams of captured onagers, and porters carrying other booty; two use packs with straps that cross the forehead. The mosaic, twenty-two inches long, adorned one side of a box.

Chariots, infantry, and prisoners, from the 'Ur Standard'.

feasting, wine goblets in their hands, while a musician plays to them on his harp.

As they are represented here and in certain other inlays, reliefs, and sculptures, with their stocky figures, hook-nosed faces, bunchy skirts, and their general lack of animation, the early Sumerians would appear to have been singularly unattractive as a people. However, artistic conventions quite alien to those we are familiar with may to some degree have dictated these appearances – as they did in Egypt where, to accentuate the most recognizable aspects of a human being, the artist showed the head in profile, the torso front on, and the legs again in profile.

On the other hand, unlike the relatively uniform and static character of Egyptian art, that of early Mesopotamia varied enormously between the extremes of realism and abstraction. The head of a bull from a harp also found at Ur, for example, is a superbly modelled sculpture that conveys to perfection the animal vitality of its subject. Still again, the famous Warka Head of a woman, fashioned in Uruk (Warka is the modern name for ancient Uruk) centuries earlier than the 'Ur Standard', in its subtle modelling and serene grace might almost be from classical Greece.

And contrasted with this life-size head, there are innumerable little carved cylinders of stone or metal used for sealing documents, whose designs, ranging from highly representational scenes to almost purely decorative arrangements, are engraved with such delicacy that we can hardly believe they were executed on such a small scale without the aid of a magnifying glass. Aside from sealing inscribed tablets these attractive and practical devices were also used to identify and protect property. They were rolled over pats of moist clay that covered the fastenings of jar and basket tops. After the impression dried and hardened the container could not be opened without damaging the sealing. From the thousands of examples that have been recovered, surely a tiny fraction of those that were made, we can judge that they represented a form of

Bull's head, also from the Royal Cemetery, which is attached to the sound box of a harp; the inlaid plaques show mythological figures, and animals as servants and musicians.

The 'Warka Head'. Originally there were inlaid eyes and brows and a finely engraved sheet of gold or copper covering the top of the head. Nearly life-size, the head is flat at the back, suggesting it may have been attached to a wooden statue.

popular art that persisted over a long period of time. They are indeed the only objects that have survived in sufficient quantity to provide a comprehensive view of Mesopotamian art over the ages. They were customarily attached to a necklace or wrist-band and were worn to the grave by their owners. Consequently every generation produced its own seals in a succession of styles that broadly display the inventiveness of the Mesopotamian designer.

Scenes such as those depicted on the cylinder seals are

This cylinder seal, made of carnelian, is incised with a characteristic motif – the hero in conflict with two wild beasts. An attacking lion, with its right paw raised, can be seen on the seal itself; on the impression the winged hero is shown with one hand holding a scimitar and the other grasping a bull.

invariably religious in nature, and occur again and again on pottery, stone vases, and stelae. In some we can recognize a familiar figure often thought to be the epic hero Gilgamesh, grappling monsters, slaying two lions with his bare hands, and, with his companion Enkidu, performing other feats described in the famous Sumerian epic. But other figures are inexplicable, and serve to demonstrate the gulf which separates us from these highly civilized people of five thousand years ago. One shows a man kneeling at the foot of a tree while a coiled snake gnaws at his genitals. 'And who', as the French archaeologist André Parrot inquires, 'will ever know why?'

Mesopotamia's political vicissitudes are reflected in its art. In the Early Dynastic period (3000–2370 B.C.) monumental palaces, rivalling the temples in size, appear as prominent features of the Sumerian cities. The newly important political and military leadership reflected in the appearance of these palaces is also indicated by the scenes depicted on the 'Ur Standard'. The fortunes of such independent city-states as Ur, Uruk, Lagash, and Eridu rose or declined in a fitful pattern of dynastic dispute, with the land subject to repeated foreign invasion, and the city-states struggling among themselves for authority over neighbouring areas. A fragment of a stele found at Lagash, the so-called Stele of the Vultures (because vultures are shown with lions, devouring naked human corpses),

Stele of the Vultures. It shows a phalanx of spearmen from Lagash advancing, behind a wall of shields, over the prostrate enemy.

records a victory of that city under its ruler Eannatum over the neighbouring city of Umma. With the help of the god Ningirsu, Umma was conquered and its armies captured. But although such conflicts were frequent they were rarely decisive. The various city-states continued to exist as separate, contending entities, recognizing no single ruler or central authority.

Meanwhile, other areas outside the lower Mesopotamian valley and other peoples who infiltrated the valley were exposed to the influence of Sumerian civilization. To the east, in the foothills of what is now southern Iran, the Elamites, both in war and in peace, were in constant contact with the urban Mesopotamian centres, and they absorbed the main elements of Sumerian culture. For century after century, Semitic tribesmen moved in from the deserts and the mountains to the west and north, intermingling with the Sumerians. These immigrants assimilated Sumerian culture so thoroughly that in time little but their language differentiated them from the original inhabitants of the valley.

The first ruler to bring the land of Sumer under one authority was Lugalzaggisi, king of Uruk. According to his inscribed records, which may be exaggerated, he extended the sway of the Sumerians from the Persian Gulf to the shores of the Mediterranean. His despotic reign was challenged and overthrown by the first great Semitic ruler of Mesopotamia, Sargon, a king whose exploits are abundantly documented. Sargon founded his capital at Akkad, the site of which has not yet been identified with certainty, although it was probably very near Babylon. If and when it is discovered it will certainly make archaeological news of great importance.

In a celebrated poem Sargon describes his lowly origin:

> Sargon the mighty king, king of Akkad, am I.
> My mother was a changeling, my father I knew not.
> The brothers of my father loved the hills.
> My city is Azupiranu, which is situated on
> the banks of the Euphrates.
> My changeling mother conceived me, in secret
> she bore me.
> She set me in a basket of rushes, with bitumen
> she sealed my lid.

She cast me into the river which rose not
over me.
The river bore me up and carried me to Akki,
the drawer of water.
Akki lifted me out as he dipped his ewer.
Akki . . . appointed me as his gardener.
While I was his gardener, Ishtar granted me her love,
And for four and . . . years I exercised kingship.

To judge from a handsome bronze head found at Nineveh and often identified as a portrait of Sargon, this great king could easily pass for a Bedouin sheikh of today, with his full, sensuous lips, strong aquiline profile, luxuriantly curled hair, and noble beard. He was evidently a born general capable of far-ranging strategic manoeuvre. He must also have had considerable armies at his command to achieve the total subjugation not only of Mesopotamia but of its neighbours. His strategic sense is evident from the manner in which he achieved his conquest. Before he attacked the Sumerian city-states to the south, he was careful to protect and consolidate his position by taking the northern towns of Mari, Assur (one of the capitals of Assyria), and Arbil. Then, in a short time, his armies overran the Sumerian cities and established him as 'King of Sumer and Akkad', the greatest to bear that name.

Sargon was more than a soldier with a knack for winning battles; he was a man of statesmanlike ability. By his conquests he incorporated the Sumerian city-states into an empire which extended westward possibly to the Mediterranean coast, eastward to Iran, and northward into Syria – an Akkadian empire which lasted about a century and a half. His energetic grandson Naram-sin pushed the frontiers into the mountains of Asia Minor, proudly boasting that he was 'King of the Four Quarters of the World'.

The Semites of Akkad had long traded with the Sumerians, they had adopted the Sumerian gods, and they had borrowed Sumerian script for writing their own language. But with the new-found political unity imposed by Sargon a fresh spirit finds expression in Mesopotamian culture. This is clearly

An Akkadian bronze, perhaps of Sargon. The eyes, inlaid with gems, were gouged out by thieves.

evident in the plastic arts. One has only to compare the lithe, fluid line of the sculptured soldiers on the Stele of Naram-sin with the rigid, hieratic figures on Eannatum's Stele of the Vultures to notice the change. Both commemorate military victories, but that is practically all they have in common. Eannatum's stele has great historical value, but Naram-sin's is a wonderful work of sculpture. With only fifteen figures, two formalized trees, a few upward-surging lines culminating in a conventional peak, the sculptor has depicted the successful attack by Naram-sin's armies on an enemy's mountain stronghold. The whole scene is alive with movement: the steady upward march of the Akkadian monarch's troops, an enemy falling back dying, another plunging from a rocky ledge, a third clasping his hands in entreaty, while towering over all stands the heroic figure of the king.

Semitic influence shows itself in other ways, for example, in

Stele of Naram-sin, Sargon's grandson. Wearing the horned helmet of the gods, the king stands alone at the summit, close to the great gods whose stars appear overhead.

This head of a divinity wearing a triple crown comes from a Sumerian city, but is Semitic in style.

more realistic portrait sculpture and the vigorous treatment of animals, especially lions and bulls. Equally remarkable is the art of the engraver. The cylinder seals of this period writhe with life: Gilgamesh grappling with a buffalo, and on another seal locking his powerful arms around a struggling lion, snapping its neck. There is an almost explosive quality in these tiny designs which foreshadows the terrifying violence of Assyrian art in later times.

A second and more permanent effect of the Akkadian conquest was the spread of the cuneiform writing system throughout the entire Near East. Akkadian became the official language of diplomacy and was used in business transactions in lands beyond Mesopotamia for many centuries. The Sumerian language was still written, but in time it became a 'learned' language, like the Latin of the Middle Ages in Europe that survived in schools and in religious rituals.

There were further dynastic changes in Mesopotamia of which only the broadest outline concerns us here. An invasion by eastern barbarians, the Guti from the Zagros Mountains, a people 'who knew not kingship', destroyed what was left of Sargon's Akkadian empire late in the third millennium. Once again there was disorganization in the land of Sumer.

The city of Lagash managed, probably by paying tribute, to escape the general chaos caused by the Guti. Its governor, Gudea, beautified Lagash with temples and palaces and with sculptures of such quality that they have become famous in our own day. Few people interested in the ancient world can not have seen these serene statues with piously folded hands, Sumerian in their static dignity and repose, but carved out of hard diorite with the skilled precision of the best Akkadian workmanship. Most of these represent Gudea himself, and like virtually all Mesopotamian portraits they were intended to show the worshipper in ceaseless vigil confronting his god in the temple. A remarkable man, he ruled Lagash at least fifteen years, but for some reason never took the title of king. In time Sumer revived under a new line of kings ruling from some of the older Sumerian cities, notably Ur and Uruk. This Neo-Sumerian Period, which covered most of the twenty-second to the twenty-first centuries B.C., marked a new golden age, in which such kings as Ur-Nammu and Dungi created enormous buildings during what is called the Third Dynasty of Ur. Of these the greatest was undoubtedly the great Ziggurat of the Moon God at Ur, the remains of which can still be seen on the lower plains of Mesopotamia. Even in decay it is impressive, but in its original glory it reared into the sky to a height of eighty feet and, with its steep flights of stairs rising to the topmost tower, it must have been comparable in

This statuette of Gudea, showing him wearing a simple robe and a woollen cap, is one of a series of more than thirty similar figures that document his governorship of Lagash. It was placed in the temple to mediate between him and the god of the city and was thought to have a power of its own: Gudea addressed one such figure, 'Statue, say to my king . . . '

splendour to the Egyptian pyramids. This achievement is even more remarkable when one considers that the largest building unit was but a small brick fifteen inches long.

Ur-Nammu was responsible for this and other buildings which lent lustre and importance to his own capital. In fact he rebuilt a substantial part of the city. His dynasty endured for more than a century, and during this Sumerian renaissance, literature flourished. It was in this period that scribes compiled many of the memorable examples of Mesopotamian literature that survive today. Weights and measures were standardized. Trade, overseas and overland, seems to have been extended even as far as the Indus Valley, indirect though this latter contact may have been.

Towards the end of the third millennium B.C. the power of the last Sumerian dynasties cracked under another invasion, this time by the Elamites from Iran and by the Amorites from the north-west, who established themselves at several places in the valley and whose cities flourished. For about a hundred years there was internecine warfare as the various city-states of Mesopotamia – Isin, Larsa, and Eshnunna in the south, Assur in the north, and Mari on the middle Euphrates – struggled for supremacy, until Babylon became the dominant power under Hammurabi in the eighteenth century B.C.

Of all these contending cities Mari is particularly interesting, for here in fairly recent years French excavators under Parrot have revealed a Mesopotamian city of the early second mil-

The palace at Mari.

lennium, in a unique state of preservation. Temples, palaces, dwelling-houses, cemeteries, superb works of sculpture, painted frescoes, and no less than twenty-five thousand cuneiform tablets have been brought to light, revealing, in Parrot's words, 'hitherto undreamt-of aspects of the Mesopotamian genius'. The plan of the great palace that has been uncovered is staggering in its complexity. It contains over two hundred and fifty rooms, ranging from the residential quarters of the king, through the scribal school (where the tablets were found),

The schoolroom at Mari, with rows of benches on which apprentice scribes sat during their lessons. Next to the benches are small baskets of clay, set into the floor to contain writing equipment.

to the stewards' offices and store-rooms. With its large central courts, its wall paintings, throne room, and maze of storage magazines, the palace at Mari is reminiscent of that at Knossos in Crete. The flounced dresses of the women shown in the brightly coloured frescoes, the spiral bands, and certain naturalistic details in the decoration are also a little like the paintings found in Minoan Crete. It would be unwise to overstress these resemblances, but they do suggest a cultural contact between the two lands.

Of all the ruined cities of Mesopotamia, Mari brings one closest to the spirit of those long-dead people. Here are the temples in which they performed those strange, complicated rites in honour of their gods; here are the sculptured figures in stone and bronze of deities, worshippers, and hieratic beasts, which once adorned their courts; here, opening out of a labyrinth of corridors, are the very rooms in which scribes made and filed their records, copied those poems and proverbs, the medical and mathematical lore, and other writings of varied interest, depositing like bees in a honeycomb, the hoarded richness of two thousand years of civilization.

On a wall of one of the courts could be seen the painting, reproduced on the opposite page, which appears to show the investiture of the king of Mari. A goddess in a narrow, flounced

Lion guarding temple-entrance at Mari.

skirt and tall head-dress presents the king, who receives from Ishtar the royal insignia. Winged, human-headed beasts, faintly recalling both the Egyptian sphinx and the Minoan griffin, flank the picture; two other goddesses pour out ritual libations, and a powerful human-headed bull stands with foot upraised. As Parrot has suggested, these strange creatures who stand guard before stylized trees may be the precursors of those cherubim of the Old Testament who forbid access to Eden and the tree of life. Thus, too, in an adjoining panel, the four streams that gush forth from vases held by two goddesses may prefigure the four rivers of Paradise. In this and other Mari frescoes the main strands of Syrian and Mesopotamian civilization meet and mingle: the rigid, hieratic formalism of Sumer, and the freer, more fluid art of Syria – in this case represented by a delightfully naturalistic picture of two men climbing a date palm, apparently oblivious to the ceremony taking place

A fresco from the palace of Mari.

On the capital of the stele on which his law code is written, Hammurabi is shown standing on a mountain-top before the sun god Shamash.

below them. But it is one thing to see these paintings in a museum or reproduced in the pages of a book; it is quite another to walk immediately across the very floor upon which this and similar rites were performed. One can do that at Mari, but not, alas, in Babylon, which rose during the early years of the second millennium B.C. to become the great capital city of the land, subduing Mari in the process.

With the decline of the great Third Dynasty of Ur the last Sumerian revival had ended, and for the following fifteen centuries Semitic races dominated the civilization of Mesopotamia. Hammurabi was the sixth king of the Semitic dynasty that was founded at Babylon in the nineteenth century B.C. It was about 1792 B.C. that this great leader came to the throne, and during the forty-three years of his reign he built an empire whose glory lingers to the present day.

Although the Sumerians ceased to constitute a significant political or military force, the culture they had developed was fused with that of the newcomers. The names of the gods were subject to change, but their functions remained the same. Babylonian temples were elaborations of Sumerian prototypes, and the deities were worshipped much as before. Babylon's city god, Marduk, became the chief god of the Mesopotamian pantheon, and his temple called Esagila became the chief sanctuary of Hammurabi's empire.

2 · The Age of Hammurabi

It used to be said of Hammurabi that he drew up the world's first legal code. At Susa, in Iran, explorers unearthed a diorite stele bearing his name and cuneiform inscriptions that set forth a comprehensive system of laws. This monolith, which had been carried to Susa by Elamite conquerors after one of their periodic raids on the Euphrates valley and which may now be seen at the Louvre in Paris, is a document of enormous interest. However, we now know that though Hammurabi may have been one of the world's greatest lawgivers and administrators, he had much earlier legal documents in the Sumerian language to draw upon. For instance, there exists the code of Lipit-Ishtar, the fifth ruler of the Dynasty of Isin, who ruled a century and a half before Hammurabi. Like Hammurabi's, this code consists of three parts – a prologue, the legal text, and an epilogue. In the prologue the king states:

> I, Lipit-Ishtar, the humble shepherd of Nippur, the stalwart farmer of Ur . . . established justice in Sumer and Akkad in accordance with the word of Enlil . . . I made the father support his children and . . . the children support their father; I made the father stand by his children and . . . the children stand by their father. . . .

There are thirty-eight known laws in this code, some of which seem entirely equitable by our modern standards. For instance:

> If a man turned his face away from his first wife . . . [but] she has not gone out of the house, his wife which he married as his favourite is a second wife; he shall continue to support his first wife. . . . If a man's wife has not borne him children but a harlot from the public square has borne him children, he shall provide grain, oil, and clothing for that harlot; the children which the harlot has borne him shall be his heirs, and as long as his wife lives the harlot shall not live in the house with his wife.

Another law code, written in Akkadian and found at Tell Obu Harmal near Baghdad, contains such practical regulations as the following:

> If the boatman is negligent and causes the sinking of the boat, he shall pay in full for everything the sinking of which he caused. . . . The wages of a hired man are one shekel of silver; his provender is one pan of barley. He shall work for one month. . . . If an ox gores another ox and causes its death, both ox owners shall divide between themselves the price of the live ox and also the equivalent of the dead ox.

Another law, that was designed to protect the interests of a returned prisoner of war, strikes a familiar note to us today:

If a man has been made prisoner during a raid or an invasion or if he has been carried off forcibly and stayed in a foreign country for a long time, and if another man has taken his wife and she has borne him a son – when he returns, he shall get his wife back.

Still earlier codes, dating at least as far back as the celebrated Sumerian king Urnammu, have survived. But Hammurabi's much larger and more comprehensive code is one of the most important documents in human history. For here, nearly two thousand years before the codification of Roman law, is an organized and comprehensive legal system governing most human activities. There are laws concerning marriage, divorce (including a husband's responsibility for his wife's debts), property rights, liability for military service, sale of wine, deposits and debts, murder and assault, theft, and the responsibility of professional men to their clients. The death sentence was imposed for theft, adultery, bearing false witness in cases involving the defendant's life, and for false accusations. There were also laws concerning agriculture, commerce, inheritance, adoption, wages, and slaves.

Praying figure. The hands and face, the noblest parts of the body, are covered with gold leaf.

A high-born Elamite woman spinning while an attendant fans her.

Although Babylonian women did not enjoy the same social status as men, their civil rights were safeguarded under Hammurabi's code. For instance, a wife whose husband neglected her could obtain a divorce provided she could prove she had lived a blameless life. A concubine who had borne children to a man who sent her away was entitled to take with her whatever dowry she had brought to him, and he was obliged to give her an income from 'field, garden, and movables' to support

her and his offspring. It is an interesting fact that the higher the social rank of the injured party, the harsher were the penalties for crime. Some of the penalties imposed on negligent professional men seem excessive but have a certain rough justice. If a doctor, through carelessness or inefficiency, caused his patient to lose the sight of an eye, he lost one of his own eyes. If a house fell on its owner, the builder of that house might be subject to death or at least to a heavy fine. However, contemporary records of lawsuits show that these more savage penalties were imposed only on rare occasions.

1
2
3
4
5
6
7

1. A nude female figure, perhaps a fertility talisman: 'If a seignior wishes to divorce his wife who did not bear him children, he shall give her money to the full amount of her marriage price and he shall also make good to her the dowry which she brought from her father's house and then he may divorce her.'

2. This street entertainer, with his performing monkeys, would be welcome at a tavern; more boisterous guests were frowned upon: 'If outlaws have congregated in the establishment of a woman wine seller, and she has not arrested those outlaws and did not take them to the palace, that wine seller shall be put to death.'

3. A married couple: 'If a woman so hated her husband that she has declared, "You may not have me", her record shall be investigated at her city council, and if she . . . was not at fault, even though her husband has been going out and disparaging her greatly, that woman, without incurring any blame at all, may take her dowry and go off to her father's house. If she was not careful, but was a gadabout, thus neglecting her house and humiliating her husband, they shall throw that woman into the water.'

4. A carpenter at work: 'If a builder constructed a house for a seignior, but did not make his work strong, with the result that the house which he built collapsed and so has caused the death of the owner of the house, that builder shall be put to death.'

5. Farmers in an orchard: 'When a seignior borrowed money from a merchant and his merchant foreclosed on him and he has nothing to pay it back, if he gave his orchard after pollination to the merchant and said to him, "Take for your money as many dates as there are produced in the orchard", that merchant shall not be allowed; the owner of the orchard shall himself take the dates that were produced in the orchard and repay the merchant for the money . . . in accordance with the wording of his tablet. . . .' (by courtesy of the Yale Babylon Collection).

6. A peasant riding upon an ox: 'If a seignior hired an ox and has caused its death through carelessness or through beating, he shall make good ox for ox to the owner of the ox.'

7. Two soldiers armed with throwsticks: 'If either a private soldier or a commissary, whose dispatch on a campaign of the king was ordered, did not go or he hired a substitute and has sent him in his place, that soldier or commissary shall be put to death, while the one who was hired by him shall take over his estate.'

These rules of law as they were applied to all social classes in everyday affairs, and the numerous records of lawsuits that have survived, help to create a more intimate impression of this vanished world than can be gleaned from the physical remains of cities and temples and the lengthy chronicles of kings. But the picture would be still far from complete without permitting the ordinary men and women of Mesopotamia to speak for themselves. For this we must turn to the little cuneiform tablets on which the folk wisdom of the people was summed up in their proverbs. So many of these axioms and adages, recast in a modern idiom, would seem immediately familiar to us of the twentieth century.

A restless woman in the house
Adds ache to pain.

Who has not supported a wife or child,
His nose has not borne a leash.

We are doomed to die, let us spend;
We shall live long, let us save.

Who possesses much silver may be happy,
Who possesses much barley may be happy,
But who has nothing at all can sleep.

The poor man is better dead than alive;
If he has bread, he has no salt,
If he has salt, he has no bread,
If he has meat, he has no lamb,
If he has a lamb, he has no meat.

You can have a lord, you can have a king;
But the man to fear is the [tax collector].

Blunt, shrewd, and cynical, these are the typical complaints and observations of civilized human beings in any epoch. Here, at this very early stage of recorded history, the inevitable drawbacks of civilized life already begin to appear – the burden of taxation, the onerousness of military service, the responsibilities of wealth, the penalties of poverty, and the trials of married life.

But other Mesopotamian writings express the highest aspirations of mankind. There is the *Epic of Gilgamesh*, the story of the first great tragic hero known to history. This superb dramatic poem, most of it originally Sumerian, antedates the Homeric epics by at least fifteen hundred years. It was transmitted through the later Babylonians and Assyrians with some modifications, surviving for thousands of years amid the rubble of vanished ancient cities until its rediscovery by archaeologists within the last century. Its hero, the mighty Gilgamesh, was a legendary king of Uruk, which claimed to be the oldest of Sumerian cities.

> The theme of that story is twofold [the modern British scholar D. G. Bridson has written], man's conquest of his environment and his yearning for immortality. . . . Out of a folk hero [the Sumerian poet and his successors] have created a symbol for mankind – transmuting a cycle of mythical adventures into a moving allegory of human courage and aspiration.

In the heroic figure of Gilgamesh are embodied the effort and striving, the terror and trials of the anonymous masses who contributed to what we label the Tell Halaf, al 'Ubaid, Uruk, and Jemdet Nasr cultures. With his close friend and companion, the formidable Enkidu, he invades the mountain forests to fell a cedar, probably an allegorical summary of the innumerable forays made by Sumerian plainsmen into the hostile uplands in quest of the wood they lacked and needed. They enter the dark ranks of cedars and confront the god Humbaba, the frightful guardian of the forest and, according to modern interpretations of the epic, a symbol of evil.

> And it was only the last barrier of the mountain forests,
> Lined up elbow to elbow like infantry,
> That was an irritation to them. . . .
> For the clustering cedars
> Made the way difficult and the going slow.
> And as a first indication of their true intentions
> In those parts, both Gilgamesh and Enkidu
> Set their hands to the axes and attacked the trees. . . .
> Then the forest god, Humbaba, struck back
> And leaping up fully armed at the first onslaught
> They fought back valiantly at the malignant anger

This detail from the sound-box of a harp discovered in one of the royal tombs at Ur and illustrated more fully on page 144 depicts Gilgamesh's conquest of two human-headed bulls.

Unleashed upon them. . . . And there was no pausing
For axes then, but swung swords began the sickling
Of all between them and that scourge . . . and the whirlwind
Scoured after them through agony of the cedar trees
Like a searching of bullwhips . . . and the thunderbolts
Bounced off the body-armour of those two heroes –
A pattern of spent sparks off an anvil. . . . And lightning crackled
About them balefully while they struck new knotted
Virulences of light out of the flame-forks
And cut them down. . . . And there was just no harness
To put upon fighting bulls like those, as they drove on –
Battering down, trampling, and crushing the indiscriminate
Heart out of that anger – forcing a final
Stranglehold of subjection upon their danger. . . .

That is Bridson's paraphrase of passages from the epic. Below, in a more literal translation of a later cycle, is the story of how Gilgamesh, fearing death and longing for immortality, approached the sun god Utu:

A detail of an Assyrian relief showing Gilgamesh holding a lion cub.

'O Utu, a word I would speak to you, to my word your ear,
I would have it reach you, give ear to it.
In the city Man dies, oppressed is the heart,
Man perishes, heavy is the heart.

I peered over the wall,
Saw the dead bodies . . . floating in the river;
As for me, I too will be served thus; verily it is so.
Man, the tallest, cannot reach heaven,
Man, the widest, cannot cover the earth.
Not yet have brick and stamp brought forth the fated end.
I would enter the "land", I would set up my name,
In its places where the names have been raised up. . . .'

'I would set up my name . . .' It is man's eternal attempt to arrest the current of time, to set a lasting stamp upon life, before he moves on to the unknown realm of the dead.

Many of the tablets from which we learn so much of Babylonian civilization, and its inheritance from ancient Sumer, date from the first half of the second millennium B.C. and are written in Sumerian cuneiform. The rest, translations and modifications of earlier versions, were found among the remains of the library formed at Nineveh by Assurbanipal, 'written down according to the original and collated in the palace' of this last great king to rule the Assyrian empire before it collapsed in the seventh century B.C.

Among those archives was found a version of the story of the Deluge, incorporated with the Gilgamesh epic but derived from independent poems which in the earliest known forms date about fifteen hundred years before the biblical story of Noah was set down, not earlier than 800 B.C., by a Hebrew scribe. This is not to suggest that the Hebrews were not familiar with the story at a much earlier date. There is every indication that the two versions stem from a common tradition. (There is no archaeological evidence of one great deluge in Mesopotamia, although the valley was subject to periodic local inundations, as Woolley discovered in his diggings at Ur, and these floods may have been disastrous within their limits.) As it was transcribed from the Assyrian archives the story reveals a close resemblance to the account in Genesis, as may be judged from the following excerpts.

Man of Shuruppak, son of Ubar-Tutu
Tear down this house, build a ship!
Give up possessions, seek thou life.
Forswear worldly goods and keep the soul alive!
Aboard the ship take thou the seed of all living things.
The ship that thou shalt build,
Her dimensions shall be to measure.
Equal shall be her width and her length.
Like the Apsu shalt thou ceil her. . . .
Ten dozen cubits each edge of the square deck.
I laid out the contours and joined her together. . . .

Then comes the dramatic description of the Deluge itself:

Consternation over Adad reaches to the heavens,
Who turned to blackness all that has been light,
The wide land was shattered like a pot!
For one day the south-storm blew,
Gathering speed as it blew, [submerging the mountains],
Overtaking the [people] like a battle.
No one can see his fellow,
Nor can one be recognized from heaven.

But the hero in his ship escapes disaster, riding the flood until at last the vessel comes to rest on 'Mount Nisir'.

Mount Nisir held the ship fast,
  Allowing no motion. . . .
When the seventh day arrived,
I sent forth and set free a dove.
The dove went forth, but came back;
Since no resting place for it was visible, she turned round.
Then I sent forth and set free a swallow.
The swallow went forth, but came back;
Since no resting place for it was visible, she turned round.

And so on until at last the flood finally recedes; a 'raven went forth and, seeing that the waters had diminished, he eats, circles, caws, and turns not round'.

Babylonian boys of good families who were sent to school to learn writing would probably have been obliged to copy such portions of the Gilgamesh epic, as well as other tales, hymns, lamentations, and wisdom literature, to familiarize themselves with the Sumerian language and the cuneiform writing system. The schoolboy also learned the timeless myths surrounding Enki, Enlil, Inanna, and other deities, much as our youngsters memorize passages of our own great classics. And probably at that age they bored him as much. But writing was the first essential step to any kind of responsible office within the hierarchy. The following, although written by a Sumerian schoolmaster for amusement, probably sums up fairly accurately the behaviour and attitude of a typical pupil, of that era as well as of ours:

[Arriving at school in the morning] I recited my tablet, ate my lunch, prepared my new tablet, wrote it, finished it; then they assigned me my oral work. . . . When school was dismissed, I went home, entered the house, and found my father sitting there. I told my father of my written work, then recited my tablet to him, and my father was delighted. . . . When I awoke early in the morning, I faced my mother and said to her: 'Give me my lunch [one hopes he said "please"], I want to go to school.' My mother gave me two 'rolls' and I set out. . . . In school the monitor in charge said to me, 'Why are you late?' Afraid and with pounding heart, I entered before my teacher and made a respectful curtsy.

The schoolboy learned how to write first by making individual signs and then by combining them in complete words. To help him, long word lists were written out on clay tablets – lists of insects, birds, stones, minerals, countries, cities, and so on, which were intended to be copied by primary students. A considerable number of these 'text-books' have been unearthed, dating from the latter half of the second millennium. Numeration was also taught as a preparation for the study of arithmetic. Addition and subtraction, multiplication and division sufficed for ordinary account keeping. Students intended for higher posts would go on to more complex mathematics, which included algebra and geometry and which were taught, as they are today, by the setting and solving of problems.

The following is one from the time of Hammurabi:

'An area A, consisting of the sum of two squares, is 1000. The side of one square is $\frac{2}{3}$ of the side of the other square, diminished by 10. What are the sides of the square?'

This leads to the equations:

$$x^2 + y^2 = 1000$$
$$y = \frac{2}{3}x - 10$$

of which the solution can be found by solving the quadratic equation

$$\frac{13}{9}x^2 - \frac{40}{3}x - 900 = 0$$

which has one possible solution: $x = 30$.

In the actual cuneiform text, however, the problem is solved by simple enumeration of the numerical steps that must be taken. In a thorough treatment of the subject, the mathematician Dirk J. Struik notes that while the Egyptians of the same period could solve simple linear equations, the Babylonians knew how to work with quadratic equations in two variables, as well as with cubic and biquadratic equations. The Babylonians had multiplication tables based on a well developed sexagesimal system, and they were the first people to indicate the value of a number by its position in a line of numbers; thus 1 followed by another 1 was equal to 61 (using the figure 60 as a unit as we would use the unit 10 in our decimal system). It was obviously much more efficient to use this system in writing numbers than it was to employ the system developed so much later by the Romans. It was of particular advantage when dealing with hundreds and thousands. Our division of the hour into 60 minutes, or 3600 seconds, and of the circle into 360 degrees is an inheritance from the sexagesimal system of early Mesopotamian times.

Mathematical skills would be needed by a student if he wished to become, say, a builder, surveyor, land appraiser, tax official, or temple astronomer – to perform any job requiring a knowledge of measurement. But he might wish to become a physician instead, in which case he would acquire a rudimentary knowledge of anatomy and surgery and an extensive catalogue of incantations and exorcisms for dealing with the demons who caused sickness. He would also learn the properties of many drugs, some of which are still used by doctors today. Over five hundred such drugs are recorded on cuneiform tablets discovered by American archaeologists at Nippur. Sumerian and Babylonian physicians understood the medicinal properties of such plants as myrtle, asafoetida, thyme, and cassia, and of such minerals as potassium nitrate and sodium chloride. They commanded enough knowledge of chemistry to be able to make filtrates, and discovered how to make a substance resembling soap, thousands of years before soap was 'invented' in Europe. The ashes of certain plants particularly rich in soda were mixed with a substance containing natural fats; the interaction between this alkali and the fat produced a soap-like ointment. Like the ancient Egyptian physicians, Sumerian doctors were able to prescribe practical therapy for cases of ophthalmia and earache.

Another subject that might have been taught was agriculture. A free interpretation of one tablet, in which a farmer gives advice to his son, directs:

> Care must be taken that their water does not rise too high over the field; when the water subsides, the wet ground must be carefully guarded against trampling oxen and other prowlers; the field must be cleared of weeds and stubble and fenced about.

Instructions are given for the breaking of the ground before ploughing, which, the young farmer learned, should be

> twice by the mattock and once by the hoe. Where necessary the hammer must be used to pulverize clods. . . . Stand over . . . labourers and see to it they [do] not shirk their work.

'Keep an eye on the man who puts in the barley seed,' the instructions continue, 'that he make the seed fall two fingers uniformly,' Then follows some careful advice about stages of growth at which the crops must be watered, on the treatment of a certain plant disease called *samana*, and about manners of harvesting, threshing, and winnowing the grain.

But these great scribal schools were more than mere vocational training centres. It has been suggested by the noted scholar Samuel Noah Kramer that they resembled modern universities; the teachers did more than teach. They were also engaged in scientific study, or in copying and editing ancient literature. But like the medieval universities of Europe, the schools were closely linked with religion. The texts copied were often the sacred myths. The stars were studied in order to determine the exact timing of the annual religious festivals.

Mathematical learning was applied to measure land, much of which probably belonged to the god of the city. And many 'graduates' of the scribal schools became priests.

The mathematical problems, the schoolboys' essays, the medical pharmacopoeia provide us with an immediate, understandable link with the past. And there are hundreds of similar links. But if the student rose to high rank in the priestly hierarchy, he would have to give equal attention to learning spells and rituals which to us seem little more than black magic, although they were just as serious and meaningful to him as the mathematical problems were. The ritual to be followed when covering the temple kettle-drum, for instance, runs on for about one hundred and fifty lines of closely written cuneiform instructions. An unblemished black bull had to be led into a certain chamber whose floor had been purified with water; it was placed on a reed mat, and its legs were tied 'with a bond made of goat's hair'. Seven loaves of barley bread, seven loaves of emmer bread, honey and cream, dates, flour, wine, beer, and milk were to be offered to the god. This however was only the beginning. Before the bull was sacrificed, the practitioners were instructed,

> You shall draw the curtains shut. On the bull you shall perform the rite of Washing the Mouth. . . . You shall whisper through a reed tube into the bull's left ear the incantation entitled *Alpu ilittu Zi attama*. . . . You shall draw a ring of *zisurra*-flour around the bull. Standing at its head you shall sing [the composition called] *Nitugki niginna* to the accompaniment of a bronze *halhallatu*. . . . Then you shall cut open that bull and start a fire with cedar. You shall burn the bull's heart with cedar . . . and *mashatu*-flour before the kettle-drum. You shall remove the tendon of its left shoulder and shall bury the body of that bull (wrapped) in a single red . . . cloth. You shall throw some *gunnu*-oil on it (and) arrange it so that its face points to the west. . . .

And so on through line after line.

It is worth noting the precision with which the rite is described. We may be sure that if one small detail were omitted the spell would be considered ineffective, just as in modern science the least deviation from correct and controlled procedure can be disastrous. The world of the Babylonians, like the worlds of the ancient Egyptians, the Hittites, the Maya, and others, was controlled by supernatural forces, and magic was employed as a practical, systematic technique to control those forces. Its aims, at least, approximated those of science, but its practices were undifferentiated from the religious observances which, in all these ancient societies, gave form to human fears and aspirations.

In one case, however, science did emerge from superstition. The Babylonians believed that the movements of the heavenly bodies controlled the life of man. The precise observations they

Discovered in a neighbouring land and dating from relatively late in Mesopotamian history, this bronze model incorporates many of the features of Sumerian religion that were paralleled throughout the Middle East. On it two nude worshippers are shown performing a religious ceremony. Beside them a small ziggurat appears; in the background is an immense jar, which has been compared to the 'brazen sea' that stood in the courtyard of Solomon's temple at Jerusalem. The pillars and sacred grove, also represented, were common symbols in Semitic religion.

made in following the progress of the planets and the stars gave rise to the science of astronomy. They identified the major constellations. They named the planets we call Mercury, Venus, Mars, Jupiter, and Saturn after the gods of their own pantheon, Nabu, Ishtar, Nergal, Marduk, and Ninurta, and watched their position in the sky to determine the will of these deities. They studied eclipses of the sun and moon and tried to predict them. If one occurred at a certain time, it might mean that agricultural prices would rise, or that the king would die and his dynasty come to an end. They developed the zodiac, as a map of the sky, the route along which the heavenly bodies travelled. With its aid, astronomers were able to cast horoscopes, and determine which days were propitious and which malign. Most of the surviving cuneiform literature treating with astronomy dates from late in Babylonian history, but the omens to which the observations are linked are very ancient, and it is evident that the Babylonians had long been attentive to the heavens.

They studied the sky with awe and foreboding, for baleful forces were always to be feared. The earth too was full of dangers, and it was to guard against them that the god Marduk, who represented order, was forced to battle anew each year against the powers of chaos, represented by the goddess Tiamat, as he had before the creation of the world. (Echoes of this ancient story occur in the Bible, when the prophets and the psalmist rejoice at God's conquest of Leviathan.) In celebration of the battle between Marduk and Tiamat, there was an annual festival in Mesopotamia, usually held in the spring before the vegetation had sprouted and while the land was still in bondage to the forces of death. At Babylon, the statues of the gods were assembled in one room in the temple of Esagila; there they conferred all of their divine powers on Marduk, so that his triumph would be assured. As the priests in the temple recited the great mythological account of Marduk's struggle, the populace fought mock battles in the streets of the town, hoping to promote the victory of their god through sympathetic magic. Marduk represented the spirit of vegetation, as well as order, and his victory would promise fertility for the forthcoming year. To help secure fertility, the king engaged in ritual intercourse within the precincts of the temple with one of the temple prostitutes, as another act of sympathetic magic. But these rituals were not enough; the gods still had to be assembled once more to ratify the favourable destiny of the city, before survival during the forthcoming year could be assured.

It was during religious festivals such as this, when strangers flocked into the towns, that the temple prostitutes were most assiduously employed. These women were divided into two classes. The 'brides of the god' were votaries who supposedly served the pleasures of the god each night. The others, ordinary temple prostitutes, accommodated the citizens of the town, and travellers. Babylonians felt no compunction about the public display of love. Indeed, the public squares and streets of the town were considered appropriate places for love-making. Harlots who made their headquarters in the taverns provided competition for the temple prostitutes. The tavern strumpets were so liberally rewarded that many amassed ample dowries, and made respectable marriages upon termination of their careers.

The 'Town of the Sacred Courtesans' was Uruk, a place sacred to Ishtar, the goddess of love, beauty, and fertility; she is only the Sumerian goddess Inanna given a Semitic name. Ishtar was the courtesan of the gods. One of her hymns proclaims that she is 'clothed with pleasure and love'.

An alabaster vase, more than three feet high, depicting a New Year's offering to Inanna, the goddess of fertility. In the top panel Inanna receives a basket of gifts from a priest. Behind her are two bundles of reeds with streamers (her attributes) and a ram supporting a figure who may represent a king of Uruk. In the centre panel men, in ritual nakedness, bear gifts to the goddess. At the bottom a motif symbolizes the abundance of nature.

Some of the elements of ancient civilization coincide with our own, and can be isolated. Such are the more practical forms of medicine, advances in astronomy, architecture, engineering, and mathematics, and those expressions of human emotions which we still can share. Other elements, however, can quickly shatter the comforting illusion that these remote ancestors of ours are 'just like us'. In many ways, they are also similar to members of primitive African or South American tribes, which still live today under the influence of witch doctors and rain makers. Certainly the culture of Babylon and Mesopotamia was sophisticated, highly organized, and basically a culture of civilized men. But it was still rooted in the practices of those primitive ancestors of the Sumerians who moved down from their hills to settle in the marshy country along the banks of the Tigris and Euphrates Rivers, six, seven, and eight thousand years ago.

3 · Kings of the World

After the death of Hammurabi, the Babylonian empire began to disintegrate. The incursion of the Kassites, an Indo-European tribe from the east, threw Mesopotamia into a turmoil. Kassite rulers conquered Babylon and all of southern Mesopotamia and controlled it for centuries, but their rule there was contested by other dynasties and other tribes. In this age of internecine warfare and foreign domination, the valley world declined culturally and politically.

With Babylon no longer an important force in the northern hills of Mesopotamia, a new Semitic people rose to power on the banks of the upper Tigris – the Assyrians, a ferocious, violent people whose profession was war. Until the time that archaeologists began to uncover the remains of their cities and palaces, knowledge of the Assyrians had been based mainly on the accounts of them in the Old Testament, mostly bitter tirades against the kings who 'laid waste all the nations'. Then in the mid nineteenth century pioneer archaeologists, such as the Frenchman Paul Emile Botta and the Englishman Austen Henry Layard, unearthed the ruins of Assyrian cities, and the western world read their reports with awe and wonder. A generation familiar with the Old Testament accounts of Assyrian conquests and the stories of their persecutions was now confronted with the visible remains of their cities, palaces, and temples and could look on images of the very people for whom the Hebrew prophets had reserved some of their harshest denunciations.

When Botta and Layard began digging and unearthed spectacular remains of great palaces, both knew that they had discovered the ruins of the greatest Assyrian cities – Nineveh and Calah – but they were not sure which was which. Nor did they know the names of the kings to whom these palaces had belonged. The decipherment of the Assyrian inscriptions, however, undertaken while these excavations were still in progress, solved the problem of identification. Botta had found Nineveh, the modern Kuyunjik, and Layard the ancient town of Calah, now called Nimrud. The cuneiform inscriptions also revealed much of the political, religious, and military aspects of Assyrian life. Together with magnificent carved reliefs, they amplified the traditional image as it is set forth in the Old Testament.

Still, the reliefs showed one scene after another of warfare. Tall, bearded kings with cruel lips are shown standing in their war chariots watching the sack of an enemy city. Prisoners are being impaled on pointed spikes; an enemy ruler, staked out on the ground, is being slowly flayed alive by men with knives. Women and children are driven away captive; headless bodies float down the river. The fiercest denunciations of the Hebrew prophets do not damn the Assyrians more effectively than some of their own pictures and inscriptions. In one of these an Assyrian king boasts:

> My officers . . . put to the sword the inhabitants, young and old, of the town . . . they did not spare anybody among them. They hung their corpses from stakes, flayed their skins and covered with them the wall of the town.

While their comrades march off laden with plunder, a contingent of Assyrian soldiers demolishes the fortifications of the burning town of Hamanu.

These savage scenes are executed with such ferocious strength, such feline suppleness of line, such violent yet disciplined force of imagination that they take the breath away. One cannot approach them without experiencing the same awe, almost terror, that they inspired at the time of their discovery over a century ago. Moreover, they may have a message for us that escaped their Victorian admirers; for here we see stated for the first time a relatively new force in civilization, a force still potent today – the power of advanced technology, ruthless discipline, and naked terror narrowly applied to one end – domination. To the Assyrians life was war; and their genius was concentrated on it. Their nobles belonged to a military caste; their armies were highly organized, and used iron weapons and such formidable engines as battering-rams and siege towers, which, when pushed up to the walls of an enemy city, enabled them to pour down fire on their enemies while they themselves were protected by armour. They added to the normal accompaniments of conquest, sack, and pillage, the calculated use of violence and terror.

Who were these people who could sever the skin from the bodies of their enemies with seeming nonchalance and yet execute such beautiful works of art?

Some time in the third millennium B.C. a stocky, dark-haired Semitic people came from the west and settled on the upper Tigris in a region that is now northern Iraq. Assur (the modern Sharqat), from which the name of these people was taken, became their chief city. It served as a northern outpost of the Sumerian civilization that dominated the valley of the two rivers, but with the fall of the Third Dynasty of Ur, around 2000 B.C., the Assyrians were able to break away from Sumerian control. In a land filled with ambitious rivals and racked by frequent foreign invasions, independence was precarious; in the eighteenth century B.C. Assyria became part of Hammurabi's empire and was ruled from Babylon, and though eventually the country regained its freedom, for centuries thereafter it was held in check by the presence of powerful kingdoms on its northern and western borders – the Mitanni and the Hittites.

About 1200 B.C., when the collapse of the Hittite empire removed the threat of opposition in the north, Assyria began to expand. During the next hundred years a succession of powerful kings held the throne. Tiglath-pileser I, one of the most memorable of these early rulers, not only rebuilt the temples and palaces of the land and restored its public works, but struck out in all directions at contesting tribes and principalities. In retaliation for earlier attacks from Babylonia he swept down into the valley and took the city of Babylon. By 1100 B.C. the Assyrians had pushed their conquests west to the Mediterranean and north to Lake Van. But soon the nation lapsed into a period of decline lasting almost two hundred years. The reasons for this decline are unknown; there are no written records and few sculptured remains. Perhaps the country lacked forceful rulers or was crowded out by its neighbours. At any rate, Babylon and the western territories were lost. It was a dark age for Assyria.

Then, in the ninth century B.C., Assurnasirpal II came to the throne, and Assyria began its march to power. This aggressive military genius reorganized the Assyrian army and led it as far as the Phoenician coast, collecting tribute from the weaker cities and prudently by-passing towns that might offer strong resistance. But the strongholds closest to the Assyrian borders could not be ignored; these were battered into submission and annexed to the king's domain. Assurnasirpal chose Nimrud, on the Tigris, as the capital of his empire and magnificently restored this ancient city.

Assurnasirpal's son, Shalmaneser III, continued his father's campaigns and waged furious war against his neighbours, especially those in the west. Twelve kings of Palestine and Syria, including Ahab the Israelite, joined in an alliance against him, but in 854 B.C. Shalmaneser defeated the coalition; he boasted that he had

> scattered their corpses far and wide and covered the face of the desolate plain with their widespreading armies. With my weapons I made their blood to flow down the valleys of the land. . . . With their bodies I spanned the Orontes as with a bridge.

Later Shalmaneser exacted tribute from Ahab's successor, Jehu, the king of Israel, in the form of 'silver, gold, a golden bowl, a golden beaker, golden goblets, pitchers of gold . . .'. The booty was listed on the side of an obelisk of black alabaster, over six feet tall, which illustrated Shalmaneser's victories and showed row after row of conquered enemies bringing tribute to him.

The Assyrian yoke was heavy, and the subject peoples were always eager to shake it off. At the end of Shalmaneser's reign twenty-seven districts revolted; under his successors other rebellions greatly weakened the Assyrian government. But rebellion against the power of Assyria rarely met with success,

The Black Obelisk of Shalmaneser III. The second register from the top shows the Israelite king Jehu bowing to the ground before Shalmaneser. The top of the obelisk is tiered in the form of a ziggurat.

and the unhappy subject nations that were rash enough to revolt found their exactions doubled and their rights limited more severely than ever. These were the lucky rebels; those less fortunate were slaughtered or, in line with a traditional policy, carried into exile. Many of the captives were enslaved and brought back to Assyria, where they laboured to build the magnificent palaces, the lofty ziggurats, and the gigantic walls that made the Assyrian cities the wonders of their time. When Israel and Damascus allied themselves once more against Assyria, in the middle of the eighth century B.C., King Tiglath-pileser III overran Israel, carrying off

40,500 of its people, together with their possessions, their spoil, their property and goods, [the king's] wife, his sons, his daughters, and his gods. . . .

Even allowing for excessive enthusiasm on the part of the ancient chroniclers, the number of captives that must have been carried off is astonishing. Tiglath-pileser's successor, Sargon II, claimed he led away as prisoners almost twenty-eight thousand inhabitants of Samaria (the capital of Israel). He banished 'the rebellious inhabitants of Carchemish . . . and brought them to Assyria', and formed 'from among them a contingent of fifty chariots, two hundred men on horseback, and three thousand foot soldiers' to add to his army. The annals of Tiglath-pileser list town after town conquered in the district of Damascus; one provided eight hundred prisoners, another seven hundred and fifty, and a third five hundred and fifty. Year after year the Assyrians pursued this policy throughout their domain, depopulating entire districts, eradicating entire nations, and carrying images of gods from their native lands.

Sargon chose Khorsabad as his capital and

built a city with the labour of the peoples of the lands which my hands had conquered . . . and I called its name Dur-Sharrukin [the citadel of Sargon].

The city was carefully planned as a huge fortified square with seven gates. In the north-west section were the palace and the ziggurat, which was probably dedicated to the god Assur. Sargon lined the walls of the palace with reliefs of enemy towns that had succumbed to his armies:

I had them set up around their interior walls; I made them objects of astonishment. Reliefs of the towns of the enemy lands, which I had captured . . . I used as adornments in those palaces, thanks to the sculptor's art.

Sargon's son Sennacherib abandoned Khorsabad and made Nineveh his capital. The palace he built there was adorned with gold, silver, copper, alabaster, ivory, and precious woods. The ceilings were white, and there were rich curtains draped

Carrying their possessions on their shoulders, a group of captives marches into exile, guarded by bowman of the Assyrian army.

back across silver bosses. In the extensive parks and gardens, mountain streams specially diverted through canals provided water for exotic trees and flowers imported from other lands. All that power could furnish and art embellish was used to beautify the new Assyrian capital.

When it rebelled against his rule, Sennacherib destroyed Babylon:

> The city and its houses, from its foundation to its top, I destroyed, I devastated, I burned with fire. The wall and outer wall, temples and gods, temple towers of brick and earth, as many as there were, I razed and dumped them into the Arahtu canal. Through the midst of that city I dug canals, I flooded its site with water, and the very foundations thereof I destroyed.

Into the palace of the king, the royal records continue, 'I entered joyfully and I opened his treasure house . . . I brought out, I counted as spoil, I seized.' It is no wonder then that the Hebrews were terrified when Sennacherib's armies marched against Judah and besieged Jerusalem, where, the Assyrian annals tell, he shut up King Hezekiah 'like a caged bird' in his royal city.

> The terrifying splendour of my majesty overcame him, and the Urbi [Arabs] and his mercenary troops which he had brought in to strengthen Jerusalem, his royal city, deserted him.

The grim story is continued in the Bible. To avoid the fate of Babylon, Hezekiah handed over to the Assyrians

> all the silver that was found in the house of the Lord, and in the treasures of the king's house. At that time did Hezekiah cut off the gold from the doors of the temple of the Lord, and from the pillars . . . and gave it to the king of Assyria.

Egypt was next. Sennacherib's son, Esarhaddon, marched into the Nile Delta and conquered Memphis, the ancient capital of the pharaohs. 'I am powerful, I am all powerful,' he exulted, 'I am a hero, I am gigantic, I am colossal, I am honoured, I am magnificent, I am without an equal among all kings. . . .' Esarhaddon was indeed without an equal among all kings. No one could withstand the mighty Assyrian armies. Nineveh was a thousand miles away from the Nile Valley, and the Egyptians tried to expel their Assyrian masters, but within a few years they had to pay the price. This time, the Assyrians travelled up the Nile to Thebes, the centre of Egyptian resistance, and sacked the city so thoroughly that it never recovered its ancient eminence.

There must have been some special quality in the character of the Assyrians that gave them their formidable prowess in war and their efficiency as rulers; perhaps it was a love of order and discipline akin to that of the later Romans. There was nothing in the nature of their homeland that could have given them special advantages; indeed, geographically, it suffered from several military disadvantages, and it may have been this very fact that forced the Assyrians to construct such cunningly devised fortifications.

In a number of other ways the Assyrians resembled the Romans of the Imperial Age. They were extremely capable engineers, devisers of ingenious military machines, and experts in siege warfare and the techniques of undermining the walls of a fortress. Their armies were well drilled and well disciplined and were organized in regular formations arranged according to arms – chariotry, cavalry, heavy infantry, light infantry, and sappers. Such tight organization was not common in armies before that time; even the mighty Persian armies of the fifth century B.C. were organized according to tribes and not the type of arms they carried.

In Assyria, as in pharaonic Egypt, the prolific royal family formed the nucleus of the ruling class; generals, governors, high court officials, and the higher echelons of the priesthood were often drawn from its ranks. Like most Oriental despots, the Assyrian king had numerous children, not only by the queen but by the women of the royal harem. Such concubines were recruited partly from among the daughters of defeated or vassal kings and princes. Conspiracies among them were frequent, since not unnaturally each wanted to advance the career or even secure the succession of her own favourite son; the queen herself does not appear to have possessed much political influence, but the queen mother often did. Such intrigues over the succession to the throne constituted one of the few weaknesses of the Assyrian system.

As the chief priest and the central figure of the cult of Assur, the king was mediator between god and man. He presented the people's cause to the god and told the will of Assur to the people. The king was totally sacred; he belonged to the god. Removed from the public, he lived an isolated existence in his palace, aloof from all except his entourage of court officials, soldiers, and slaves, and, of course, the women of the harem. Visiting dignitaries often received no more than a glimpse of his figure, far off in the throne room. When they were allowed into his presence, they could address him only after kissing the ground at his feet.

Nevertheless, this aloof king was never very far from the sights and sounds of the battlefield. Even on those ceremonial occasions when he feasted among his nobility, sculptured scenes of battle, conquest, and the hunt were visible in the flickering light of massive torches. These were the subjects most beloved by the Assyrian aristocracy. Looking at such reliefs, in which battering-rams pound the walls of enemy cities, or the king in his war chariot leads his spearmen to victory, Assurbanipal and his predecessors must have recalled with pride that, as the inscriptions state, an Assyrian king shared fully in the hardships and dangers of a campaign. One such inscription has been translated:

> I had pitched my camp at the foot of the Nipur mountain and with my select bodyguard and my indomitable warriors I advanced like a strong wild ox. Gorges, mountain streams, and cataracts, dangerous chasms I traversed in my palanquin. If it were too precipitous for my palanquin I proceeded on foot. Like a young gazelle I ascended the high mountain peaks in pursuit of [the enemy]. Whenever my knees gave way under me I sat down on a rock and drank cold water from a water-skin to quench my thirst.

The contrasting picture of the king presiding in godlike state over his grovelling courtiers and the king leading his warriors through wild and rugged country is arresting. In Egypt such expressions of military ardour were sometimes – though not invariably – conventional, but one feels that if an Assyrian monarch were unable to demonstrate his soldierly qualities he probably would not have remained king for long.

The native subjects of the king may be divided into three

classes corresponding roughly to the aristocracy, the freemen, and the slaves. From the aristocracy the king chose all of his dignitaries – governors, priests, court officials, and so on. Occasionally women filled some of these high positions. There are records that tell of women who governed provinces, and one Assyrian queen, Sammuramat, prototype of the legendary Semiramis, ruled as co-regent for a time and was immortalized by Herodotus as a great conqueror who led the Assyrian armies to victory after victory.

The cuneiform tablets discovered in the ruins of the Assyrian cities tell us much about the middle classes. These classes included not only what we would call professional men, such as bankers and scribes, but also many kinds of craftsmen. Though each profession had a different status, all appear to have been organized into guilds. Every freeman had to pay taxes, generally in the form of produce or labour. All fit males of this class were liable for military service; besides their standing army of regular troops, the Assyrian rulers recruited mass levies in time of war. A man of means, however, could avoid service by providing a slave to replace himself.

There were merchants who must have profited greatly from the caravan trade in order to afford the twenty-five per cent interest that was charged for loans. These merchants traded in slaves, horses, camels, and manufactured goods, especially fabrics. Gold, silver, and copper were the metals used for exchange, and by the eighth century B.C. coinage had come into use. A very ancient Assyrian trading station dating from early in the second millennium was discovered at Kultepe in Anatolia, with its cuneiform business documents and letters still preserved in their files. From these it is clear that at an early date Assyrian trade was highly organized and extended over a large area; Kultepe was obviously an entrepôt at which Assyrian manufactured goods were traded for copper and other valuable metals of Anatolia.

In late Assyrian times there was a large class of agricultural slaves attached to the land; if the farm they lived on were sold, they went along to its purchaser. Most slaves, however, lived in the cities and were engaged in domestic work. Despite their status, slaves could still own personal property, and there were

As his court musicians entertain him and birds in the tree-tops chirp in accompaniment, King Assurbanipal reclines on a couch within his garden, enjoying a peaceful dinner. His wife sits beside him on a high, throne-like chair. The scene is not completely idyllic; at the far left of the relief the severed head of an Elamite king can be seen hanging from a tree.

some who possessed land of their own. Their lot on the whole was comfortable; indeed, the condition of the slave in Assyria seems to have been better than in any other ancient society.

Life at the court of the king is easier to visualize than the existence of the common people. Because of the lengthy personal accounts recorded by the king, all his habits and surroundings can be re-created. This is particularly true of Assurbanipal, the last of the great Assyrian kings. During his reign, from about 669 to 626 B.C., the splendour of the empire reached its greatest height. Assurbanipal continued the embellishment of the royal capital at Nineveh. Its mighty palaces were enriched with precious metals and fine woods, and its parks and gardens were adorned with exotic flowers and trees. It must have been a rich jewel in that sombre landscape. Visitors to the mud-brick mounds that are Nineveh today find difficulty in imagining it as it was, when its streets and courts were thronged with richly dressed, bejewelled women and swarthy men with square-cut, curling beards, when the smartly turned-out Assyrian troops, armed with spears and bows, clattered past echoing palace walls as they escorted some great official in his chariot through the town.

King Assurbanipal rides in his ceremonial chariot.
The pages behind him carry fly whisks to chase insects away from the royal presence.

Another in the series of reliefs illustrating Assurbanipal's lion hunt.

A wounded lion attacks King Assurnasirpal as he rides across the hunting field. Beside the royal chariot another beast lies dying.

At the court and in the homes of the powerful there was wealth and luxury. Singers and musicians entertained guests at royal and noble banquets, as we can see from the depictions on stone reliefs. But the king was probably more stately and austere than in Sumer or even in Egypt. Underlying all this richness and sophistication one senses uneasily the overwhelming power of those kings; that power informs the hundreds of sculptured scenes, carved on massive blocks of stone, that are the most impressive and most durable legacy of the Assyrians.

The best of these reliefs date from the time of Assurbanipal, when the tribute of hundreds of foreign towns poured into the royal coffers to pay for the adornment of Nineveh. On them, the king, larger than his courtiers, grasps a lion by its mane and plunges his sword into its chest, or appears as the awesome conqueror, with abject foreigners under his sword. Assurbanipal's ferocious war against the Elamites is depicted at length, the enemy fleeing in panic from Assyrian warriors, whose spears and arrows are everywhere. In all this, there is that astonishing muscularity and vigour so characteristic of Assyrian art.

The bronze gates of Balawat show the inhabitants of the island of Tyre rowing ashore with tribute for the king of Assyria. In the lower register, chariots and infantrymen leave a circular camp-site [left] to attack an enemy town.

Certain motifs appear over and over again – chariots and horses, bowmen in the midst of battle, cities besieged, captives being led into exile. The subject matter, with its continual obsession with warfare, its armies endlessly ravaging nation after nation, is ruthless, often to the point of monotony. But there are more genial aspects to the art of Assyria. The colossal winged bulls that guarded the entrances to the palace courtyards were overpowering; they stood some sixteen feet high. Still, they represented protective geniuses, and their benevolence is manifest. Among the delicate ivories found at Nimrud, mostly Phoenician in style, are some done by Assyrian craftsmen, revealing that they were equally capable of working with more peaceful themes.

It is hard to believe that merely fourteen years after the reign of Assurbanipal, 'the great king, the legitimate king, the king of the world', the Assyrian empire collapsed. One possible explanation for the downfall might be that Babylonia, as well as many other captive territories, had never wholly bent under the yoke of Assyria, but had continued to resist its domination. Undoubtedly Assyria's financial resources had been drained by the necessity of suppressing rebellion. Another reason could be

Winged bull with human head. Sculptors gave these statues five legs so that they would look realistic when viewed from either the front or side.

An Assyrian ivory representing a cow and calf in a lotus thicket.

that the frequent foreign wars had taken a great toll of Assyria's fighting men. After a while the incessant demand for more native soldiers to fill the army's ranks could not be met, and the kings were forced to rely on their subject nations for soldiers. Inevitably, this led to a deterioration in the quality and the loyalty of Assyria's forces.

'Woe to the bloody city!' the Hebrew prophet Nahum had proclaimed against Nineveh.

> It is all full of lies and robbery; the prey departeth not; the noise of a whip, and the noise of the rattling of the wheels, and of the prancing horses, and of the jumping chariots. The horseman lifteth up both the bright sword and the glittering spear: and there is a multitude of slain, and a great number of carcasses. . . .

After a three-month siege by the combined forces of Babylonians and Medes, the Assyrian capital finally fell in 612 B.C., suffering the same fate that the Assyrians themselves had so often meted out to other proud capitals. Assyria was divided between its two conquerors. The Medes took the region east and north of the Tigris River, the Babylonians, under the leadership of Nebuchadnezzar, the region to the west and south, and with it the control of a vast empire.

About twenty-four hundred years ago the Greek traveller

Herodotus, having made the difficult journey from the Mediterranean coast across the mountains and deserts of Syria and then down the Euphrates, stood entranced looking down at the streets of Babylon. He was not a naïve, inexperienced visitor, but a widely travelled and cultivated man. He had, in his time, visited most of the eastern Mediterranean countries, including, of course, Greece and the Greek islands (he was born in Asia Minor). He had coasted along the shores of Palestine, toured North Africa, examined the pyramids of Egypt, and had long discussions with the priests of Memphis. He had passed through the Dardanelles, cruised along the western shores of the Black Sea as far as the mouth of the Dnieper in modern Russia, and studied the customs of the Scythians of the steppes. If ever there was a 'man of the world' in the literal sense, it was Herodotus. He was not a man who was very easily impressed.

This is part of what he wrote in the fifth century B.C. concerning Babylon:

> Babylon lies in a wide plain, a vast city in the form of a square with sides nearly fourteen miles long and a circuit of some fifty-six miles, and in addition to its enormous size it surpasses in splendour any city of the known world. It is surrounded by a broad, deep moat full of water, and within the moat there is a wall fifty royal cubits wide and two hundred high. . . . On the top of the wall they constructed, along each edge, a row of one-roomed buildings . . . with enough space between for a four-horse chariot to turn. There are a hundred gates in the circuit of the wall, all of bronze with bronze uprights and lintels. . . . There is a fortress in the middle of each half of the city: in one the royal palace surrounded by a wall of great strength, in the other the temple of Bel [or Marduk], the Babylonian Zeus.

Admittedly there are serious discrepancies between Herodotus' description and the excavated remains – so many, in fact, that it has been doubted whether the Greek historian had ever been to Babylon. But this is an extreme view and not generally accepted. His description of the city seems reliable in most respects, although the measurements he gives are exaggerated. The excavations of Babylon at the beginning of this century, by a German expedition under the direction of Robert Koldewey, established the circumference of the walls surrounding the city as about eleven miles; but Herodotus' estimation of fifty-six may have included the walls of the near-by town of Borsippa, which stands directly to the south on the Euphrates. The thickest of these walls was found to be only thirteen feet wide, a considerable difference from the figure of eighty feet reported by Herodotus. Since most of the walls have disappeared or have been greatly reduced in height, we have no means of checking whether they were originally three hundred and forty feet high, as Herodotus claimed; but it has been pointed out that walls that high would require a base far wider than thirteen feet to support them.

There are other difficulties in reconciling Herodotus' account with the visible remains. The city appears to have been rectangular, not square in plan, and to have contained three main districts, not two, as Herodotus claimed. Within the section called Babil stood one of the large palaces of the renowned king Nebuchadnezzar. The district of Amran, to the south, contained Esagila, the temple of Marduk, adjoining the lofty ziggurat Etemenanki, the 'tower of Babel'. Between these two districts was the centre of the city, the Kasr, where stood the main palace of Nebuchadnezzar and its Hanging Gardens, the great Gate of Ishtar, and the celebrated Processional Way. This road was flanked on each side by cliff-like walls of gleaming glazed tiles, on which enormous reliefs of lions glowered down on the visitor as he approached the great temple of Marduk. Various of these, discovered by Koldewey, stand in museums around the world, and in the Berlin Museum is a reconstruction of the Ishtar Gate that incorporates several of the reliefs of bulls and dragons that decorated the original structure.

Built on a mound high above the city, Nebuchadnezzar's palace with its many courtyards must have been an overwhelming sight. In the throne room was a splendid wall relief of glazed bricks, representing a procession of yellow lions. Above them were garlands of colourful flowers and tall graceful columns shown against a background of rich blue tile.

> I laid the foundation of the new palace firmly [the king wrote] and built it up mountain-high with bitumen and baked bricks. Huge

cedars I caused to be laid for its roof, door leaves of cedar mounted with copper, thresholds and hinges made of bronze I fitted to its gates. Silver, gold, precious stones, all that is costly and glorious, wealth and goods, ornaments of my exaltedness I stored within it, an immense abundance of royal treasures I accumulated in it.

In the north-east corner of the palace, overlooking the Ishtar Gate and as if suspended between the earth and the sky, were the so-called Hanging Gardens, which the Greeks named one of the Seven Wonders of the World. In the course of his excavations Koldewey came upon a large vaulted structure, the roof of which was protected by an unusually thick layer of earth. In one of the chambers underneath the roof he found a curious well consisting of three shafts side by side, the largest being in the centre.

I can see no other explanation [wrote Koldewey] than that a mechanical hydraulic machine stood here, which worked on the same principle as our chain pump, where buckets attached to a chain work on a wheel placed over the well.

Though still not proved, it could well be that this substructure supported the gardens, that the trees and lawns may have been planted on the thick layer of earth and kept moist by water pumped up from below. But there is another equally fascinating feature of this building; perhaps the Babylonians had learned to defeat the torrid heat of their summers by cooling the air. Koldewey concluded:

The air that entered the chambers [surrounding the gardens] . . . through the leaves of the trees must have been delightfully cooled by the continuous watering of the vegetation. Possibly the palace officials did a great part of their business in these cool chambers during the heat of summer.

The word *hanging* is in any case a misnomer, the result of faulty translation. The term used by the Roman historian Quintus Curtis Rufus is *pensiles*, which could mean either 'hanging' or 'in the form of a balcony'. What made the Babylonian balconies one of the Seven Wonders of the World was the fact that they had extensive gardens laid out upon them. Not that the Romans ever saw them. Long before they appeared in Mesopotamia Babylon had been deserted and its buildings were crumbling to dust.

The city that Herodotus and other Greek travellers saw was mainly the work of Nebuchadnezzar and his successors of the seventh and sixth centuries B.C. In those years it must fully have deserved the description accorded it by St John the Divine in the Book of Revelation:

> That great city Babylon, that mighty city! . . . The merchandise of gold, and silver, and precious stones, and of pearls, and fine linen, and purple, and silk, and scarlet . . . all manner vessels of ivory, and all manner vessels of most precious wood, and of brass, and iron, and marble . . . ointments, and frankincense, and wine, and oil . . . and horses, and chariots, and slaves, and souls of men.

What stands out very clearly is that the Babylonians, from the time of Hammurabi onwards, derived much of their wealth from trade and commerce. They were a nation of merchants. The units of currency that occur so often in the Old Testament, the talent and the shekel, are Babylonian. A great many of the cuneiform tablets found at Babylon, Nineveh, Ur, Nippur, and other Mesopotamian sites are bills, receipts, business contracts, accounts, and invoices. Babylon's caravans moved along much-travelled routes to and from Iran, Syria, Palestine, and Asia Minor. Its ships sailed down the Euphrates and through the Persian Gulf to Telmun, to bring back the produce of Arabia and India. Its rafts, or *keleks*, made of reeds and inflated skins, floated down to Babylon bringing minerals from Armenia. Among its own exports were barley, dates, and wools, and woven stuffs and other manufactured products. But despite their wealth the Babylonians were not able to control their empire for very long.

Nabonidus, the last king of Babylon, who reigned from 555 to 538 B.C. was of Aramaean origin and chose to worship his native god, Sin, rather than the Babylonian Marduk. When the priests of Marduk, and eventually the people, turned against him, he withdrew to the town of Harran and left his son Belshazzar in charge of the capital. It was while Belshazzar was ruling in Babylon that Cyrus the Persian succeeded in the apparently impossible task of taking the city. Despite the protection of its enormous walls, despite the fact that the citizens had provisions and water to withstand a long siege, Babylon fell. The Euphrates ran through the city, but it was of such a depth as to be unfordable. So the Persian king, Herodotus reports, employed 'all his noncombatant troops' in digging a canal that drained off the river into a marsh.

> The Persian army which had been left at Babylon for the purpose entered the river . . . and making their way along it, got into the town. If the Babylonians had learned what Cyrus was doing or had seen it for themselves in time, they could have let the Persians enter and then . . . caught them in a trap and wiped them out. But as it was they were taken by surprise. . . . Owing to the great size of the city the outskirts were captured without the people in the centre knowing anything about it; there was a festival going on, and even while the city was falling they continued to dance and enjoy themselves, until hard facts brought them to their senses. That, then, is the story of the . . . capture of Babylon.

Herodotus certainly could not have read the Hebrew chronicles of that disaster. Yet the latter part of his calm historical narrative confirms the impassioned poetic description of the prophet Daniel, an unwilling guest of Belshazzar at that festival:

> Belshazzar the king made a great feast to a thousand of his lords, and drank wine before the thousand. Belshazzar, while he tasted the wine, commanded to bring the gold and silver vessels which his father Nebuchadnezzar had taken out of the temple which was in Jerusalem; that the king and his princes, his wives and his concubines, might drink therein. They drank wine, and praised the gods of gold, and of silver, of brass, of iron, of wood, and of stone.

(As noted, Nabonidus, not Nebuchadnezzar, was the father of Belshazzar.)

The greatest of the 'false gods' was Marduk, who had assimilated the characteristics of the Sumerian god Enlil. All the deities worshipped in Babylon, though they bore Babylonian names, were in fact directly linked with the gods and goddesses who had been honoured in Mesopotamia for more than two thousand years. At the time, the ancient religion could not have seemed more impregnable; it was as firmly established as the temple that Nabopolassar had rebuilt for Marduk, which, in the words of that king, had 'its foundations firm to the bosom of the Underworld'.

Yet the world was changing; the foundations of the old faiths were crumbling, and the Hebrew poet, with prophetic insight, knew that one of the heaviest blows at those foundations was being delivered that night. While Belshazzar 'drank wine before the thousand', Cyrus' men waded through the shallow river and burst in upon the unsuspecting city.

> In the same hour came forth fingers of a man's hand, and wrote . . . upon the plaster of the wall of the king's palace: and the king saw the part of the hand that wrote. . . . And this is the writing that was written, *Mene, mene, tekel, upharsin*. . . . Thou art weighed in the balances, and art found wanting. Thy kingdom is divided, and given to the Medes and Persians.

So Babylon fell to the Persians, who did not destroy it, as Sennacherib had done, but preserved the city as part of their Achaemenian Empire. Later it rebelled and was retaken by the Persians under Darius. Even then, though its defences were thrown down, the Persians spared Babylon, so that Herodotus, when he went there in the next century, could still see much to admire. A century still later, when Alexander the Great passed that way, he planned to rebuild and revive Nebuchadnezzar's capital, making it one of the principal towns of his eastern empire. But after his death, when the Seleucid Dynasty inherited this part of Alexander's dismembered dominions, Babylon was abandoned and deserted. But its ancient civilization, its gods, its literature, and its cuneiform writing survived down to the beginning of the Christian era; and by then elements of its culture had passed almost imperceptibly into that of Greece, which has transmitted them to us.

The picture that remains is that of Herodotus, one of the earliest representatives of our Western civilization, looking down at this moribund relic of the ancient east. He had never heard of Sumer and Akkad, let alone Tell Halaf, al 'Ubaid, or Uruk. But his description of Babylon in the fifth century B.C. might well have been applied, in broad outline, to a Sumerian city built two thousand years earlier. Both had the same basic structure – rings of defensive walls, the palace of the king, and the temple and towering ziggurat of the great deity. Beyond the walls he could see fields irrigated and cultivated by the same methods the Sumerians had developed.

The ruins of the West Gate can still be seen at Babylon.

Today Babylon and the other once-great cities of Mesopotamia are little more than desolate, dun-coloured mounds of dried mud, surrounded for the most part by desert or scrubby little fields. Around them, abandoned irrigation works – silted canals, mounds, and ditches – are all that remain where thousands once laboured in fields of waving wheat and barley for the glory of their gods. Yet the world these people created lives on and not only in their written records and in the buildings and artifacts restored by the patient labours of archaeologists. It survives within our minds, even among those who have never heard of Sumer or Akkad. Every time we look at a watch or a compass, or use a protractor, we are thinking like the Babylonians, in multiples of sixty. When we study star maps or, at a less scientific level, read a column on astrology in a popular newspaper, we share something with the Sumerian and Akkadian priests who watched the cloudless heavens from their temple roofs. For all who read the Bible, the world of ancient Mesopotamia is reflected in the voices of the Old Testament prophets and psalmists. The more we learn of the world of the Sumerians and their cultural descendants in Babylon and Assyria, the more we understand our debt, spiritual and material, to the civilization that first flourished in the Land Between the Rivers.

3 The Valley of the Indus

The story of the primitive founders of the Indus Valley civilization, who ventured down from their mountain homelands and tamed the dangerous, inhospitable, but fertile valley of the great Indus River, has all the elements of a heroic saga. Yet compared with the civilizations of Egypt and Mesopotamia, the Indus Valley culture, which arose about 2500 B.C., lacks apparent glamour. As far as we know, the Indus people created no poetic myths and chronicles, as did the Sumerians. We have no Indus equivalent of the great epic of Gilgamesh and Enkidu; the names of their gods and kings (if indeed they had kings), their sages and heroes are unknown. Only scatters of pottery and tools – 'culture spreads' – patiently traced by archaeologists from the valley to the mountains provide evidence of unremitting work and struggle.

From this civilization, which lasted for about a thousand years, there are substantial remains of two great cities – Harappa and Mohenjo-daro – and numerous smaller sites covering an immense area, from the Simla hills (the foothills of the Himalayas) in the Punjab to Sutkagen-dor near the coast of the Arabian Sea, a total distance of some one thousand miles. South-east of the river's mouth, other evidence of the Indus culture has been found near the coast as far as the Gulf of Cambay, the broad inlet just above the modern city of

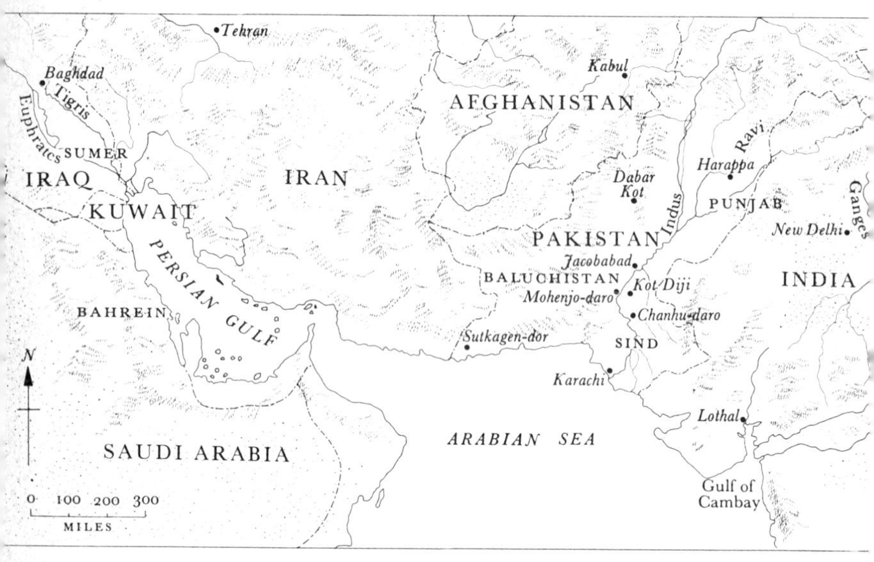

The Indus Valley.

Bombay; and in 1958 typical Indus artifacts were found within thirty miles of New Delhi, far beyond the frontiers of jungle and desert, which archaeologists thought would have prevented the culture's eastward expansion.

It is an absorbing story, with the added appeal of relative newness. The Indus Valley civilization – frequently called the Harappa civilization – is one of the most recently discovered cultures of the ancient world. Only in 1921, when an Indian archaeologist began to unearth the buried remains of Harappa, did it become evident that the Indus could take its place beside the Nile and the Tigris-Euphrates as the begetter of a great riverine culture of the ancient world – a culture that might be traced back almost forty-five hundred years into the past. Part of its fascination lies in the grim fact that it appears to have foreshadowed some of the economic features of the totalitarian state. Admittedly there is insufficient evidence on which to form definite conclusions, but the barrack-like buildings, the huge granaries, and the raised platforms on which rows of workmen pounded grain all suggest a life of controlled communal activity. This is one interpretation, and it is not universally shared by archaeologists, but only further study and excavation can prove it true or false.

Much still remains to be learned. No royal tombs have been discovered. The Indus Valley people had a writing system, but we cannot read the writings that have been uncovered. Our knowledge of their social customs is as uncertain as what we know of their origins. Even the reason for the collapse of their long-established culture is not known with certainty, though there may be clues in the *Rig-Veda*, a collection of Hindu religious hymns that, like Homer's *Iliad* and *Odyssey*, may prove to have a historical basis.

The *Rig-Veda* is the sage of the Aryans, Indo-European invaders who swept down from the north-western hills to the Punjab about 1500 B.C. and eventually settled throughout India. Their greatest god was Indra, from whom the subcontinent takes its name. It used to be assumed that the land these warriors seized was, before their coming, a barbarous country to which they brought the light of civilization. But scholars note that one of Indra's names was *puramdara*, 'fort destroyer'. In one passage he is described as destroying ninety forts; in another he 'rends forts as age consumes a garment'. The word *pur*, meaning 'rampart' or 'stronghold', occurs frequently in the *Rig-Veda;* some are built of stone (*asmamayi*), others of mud brick.

What were these forts? Until this century there was not one known building in all India that could be dated earlier than 500 B.C. Historians generally dismissed the 'forts' as mere stockades, such as primitive people might raise for protection. But with the first excavation of Harappa, archaeologists began to read the *Rig-Veda* in a new light. The Indus Valley, it now appeared, had been the seat of a major civilization for a thousand years before the Aryan invasion. The forts that Indra's people stormed may well have been Harappa, Mohenjo-daro, and the other Indus cities. Perhaps Indra himself was the human leader of the conquering race, later deified by his grateful followers. If so, we know what brought the Indus civilization to its violent end, after it had been in existence for roughly a thousand years.

'What is most important in history?' asks a distinguished archaeologist. 'Is it ideas or faith, technology or great men, property systems or geography?' The archaeologist, faced with a society whose few surviving written records are still undeciphered and whose oral tradition has been lost, has to make what he can of what does remain, and in the case of the Indus Valley people the remains are scanty. We know nothing about their ideas or faith, or about their great men, and can only guess at their economic system. One is left with technology and geography. The lay reader may be surprised at what has been learned despite these handicaps. In fact, the revelation of the Indus Valley civilization is a classic example of what archaeology can achieve by the interpretation of material remains – non-written evidence – alone.

Archaeologists had long been intrigued by the huge mounds of mud brick at Harappa, a site near the former course of the Ravi River, one of the chief tributaries of the Indus. The first excavations were carried out by Rai Bahadur Daya Ram Sahni, a young Indian on the staff of Sir John Marshall, at that time Director-General of Archaeology in India. In his preliminary excavations Sahni found a number of tiny seal stones bearing animal designs of great beauty, together with what was evidently some form of picture writing that bore no resemblance to any known script.

Precise dating was impossible, but from tools and other objects discovered deep in the mound it was clear that the builders of this buried city, whoever they were, had lived before the coming of the Aryans. They had reached only a chalcolithic stage of development, which was an intermediate stage between the ages of stone and bronze, when implements fashioned from both materials were in use. (In Mesopotamia and Asia Minor the Chalcolithic Period lasted for about two thousand years before the beginning of the Bronze Age in about 3500 B.C.) The lowest level of the Indus culture at Harappa – that is, the earliest level – has since been given a provisional dating of about 2500 B.C.

The Harappa mound was difficult to excavate, being partly overlaid by the modern village; moreover, in the nineteenth century it had been heavily plundered for ballast by the builders of the Lahore–Multan railway. Despite these handicaps the excavators were able to establish some of the principal features of what had been a city of some three miles in circumference. Certain of these features were unique and have no parallel outside India. Most remarkable was a great citadel roughly 460 yards long and 215 yards wide, rising high above the lower city and surrounded by a mighty baked-brick wall, 45 feet wide. There were projecting bastions, ramps, and gates protected by guardrooms. This grim military structure frowned down on the city and the plain beyond.

To the north of the citadel, the archaeologists came upon a complex of buildings that they eventually identified as a double row of barrack-like dwellings, and a further double range of huge granaries. Near by were remains of eighteen circular brick work platforms, each with a central hole in which had stood a heavy wooden mortar. Fragments of straw and barley found in these holes indicate that the platforms had been used for pounding grain. There is nothing unfamiliar in the presence of threshing floors; a similar system of pounding grain with pestles is used in Kashmir today. What may be significant is that the work was evidently done under the supervision of watchers in the citadel. This and the uniform rows of barracks strongly suggest government planning and control of at least this aspect of the economy.

Circular brick threshing-floor at Harappa.

The granaries, a little to the north of the work platforms, had been of remarkable size. They were arranged in symmetrical rows, and the floor of each was supported on low walls with projecting air-vents, to allow the air to circulate and thus keep the grain dry. The total floor space of the complete system of granaries, each of which measured fifty by twenty feet, amounted to twelve thousand square feet. In view of the vast size and the apparent systematic planning of the whole complex, the uniformity of the buildings, and the dominating presence of the citadel, it is difficult to escape the conclusion that these were state granaries. In addition, the excavators found evidence that the granaries were entered to the north from the banks of the river, which suggests that the grain was drawn from distant as well as near-by areas.

More substantial evidence came to light when another member of Marshall's staff, R. D. Banerji, excavated the city mound at Mohenjo-daro, nearly four hundred miles to the south-west, in the province of Sind. Here there were few overlying buildings, and the excavating team, employing hundreds of workers, was able to strip the great mound of the accretions of some thirty-five hundred years and reveal a sight that astonished archaeologists, who flocked to see it.

For there was no doubt this time. Here, bared to the fierce Indian sun after lying in darkness for probably thirty-five centuries, lay the skeleton of a vast city that had once swarmed with ant-like activity. The comparison with ants, though banal, can hardly be avoided. Even the architect's plan of Mohenjo-daro reminds one of the type of many-chambered structures these insects construct. Apart from the citadel, a great bath, and a granary, there is little evidence of monumental architecture. Temple and palace there may have been, though they have not been definitely identified. Instead we see hundreds of small buildings, many of uniform size and construction, laid out on a gridiron plan. The main thoroughfares were roughly thirty feet wide, but the houses, with their windowless outer walls, fronted on narrow lanes that appear to have been deliberately dog-legged in order to break the force of the prevailing winds.

Some of the houses were of reasonable size and planned with

If Mohenjo-daro had a temple, it might logically have stood at the highest point of the citadel. That area is today covered by a Buddhist shrine, or *stupa* [background, left], erected over two thousand years later.

a feeling of spaciousness and dignity. A typical example has a porter's lodge at the entrance, and a passage leading to a pleasant courtyard that opens on to several rooms. Most of these buildings were of baked brick faced with plaster, and may have had an upper storey approached by stairways that still survive. They contained bathrooms and latrines, often on two floors. Everywhere is clear evidence of controlled urban planning; earthenware drains encased in brick – one of the distinguishing marks of the Indus Valley civilization – carried sewage away from the houses, and numerous inspection holes show that they were regularly cleared.

There were many shops, including one that contained sockets in the floor, possibly for wine jars, and that may have been a restaurant; numerous wells, both public and private;

and small 'sentry boxes' that may have been for police or watchmen. As Sir Mortimer Wheeler, the great student of the Indus Valley civilization, has remarked, the whole plan of the city is evidence of 'middle-class prosperity with zealous municipal supervision'.

And, as at Harappa, Mohenjo-daro (the name may mean 'the hill of the dead') had its towering citadel and state granary, though in this case they were better preserved. The citadel was built on an artificial mound about forty feet high, protected by a massive wall of mud brick with towers reinforced by timber. Within was a huge bath or tank, made watertight with mortar, bitumen, and four layers of brick. Near-by buildings, it has been suggested, may have belonged to a college of priests, but this is as yet unproved. The conspicuous emphasis on bathing, probably for purposes of purification, brings to mind current Hindu religious ritual; this and other evidence suggest that certain features of the Indus Valley civilization did indeed survive the Aryan invasion. (Religious practices in particular may have been adopted by the conquerors and handed down to present-day Indian culture.)

The citadel and the state granary at Mohenjo-daro were as elaborate as those at Harappa, and so similar in construction as to make it appear that these were the twin capitals of a common civilization, even though they were four hundred miles apart. No Indus cities of comparable size have since been found, but the numerous villages and small settlements stretching from the hills in Simla to the coast, and for a considerable distance along that coast, all bear the unmistakable marks of the Indus culture – the characteristic seals, often with pictographic writing, the triangular terracotta 'cakes' (the purpose of which is not known), the painted pottery, the tools, weapons and architecture. The total area is more than twice that of Egypt or Mesopotamia.

It was a truly indigenous culture, owing nothing to Egypt, and except perhaps for the germinal concept of organized communal life, owing little directly to Mesopotamia; however, seals with Sumerian motifs, as well as beads, ornaments, and occasionally tools, prove that there were at least trading contacts with the Land Between the Rivers. In an age when no

Harappan seal stamp showing man holding two animals at bay.

place on earth is more than two days' journey away, it is difficult to comprehend, a world in which three great civilizations – Egypt, Sumer, and the Indus Valley – could grow up independently, each with its own characteristic art, technology, and religious and social system. The area in which these three self-contained worlds developed could be spanned by a jet plane in about seven hours.

Where did the founders of the Indus Valley civilization come from? This question has been partially answered, though much remains to be discovered. They were not colonists from the already developed civilization of Sumer; the evident differences between the two cultures are too great to admit that possibility. But neither could they have come from the east or south; the earliest cultures of central India and the Ganges area are later than that of the Indus. Thus the search is narrowed down to the border regions of Baluchistan and eastern

Iran. We have already noted how some of the peoples who founded the civilization of Sumer came from the western mountain valleys of Iran; it now seems likely that on the eastern slopes of the Iranian massif lived other agricultural communities, and it was among these that some of the earliest Indus Valley settlers originated.

To reach the fertile Indus, such Iranian immigrants would have had to traverse Baluchistan or Afghanistan. Intelligently directed, systematic digging in those areas might well yield interesting evidence. Here, surely, lies a promising field for archaeologists, as suggested by Sir Mortimer Wheeler, who apparently awaits the development of such a programme with some impatience.

> The high mound of Dabar Kot in the Zhob Valley of northern Baluchistan [he notes] exhibits in its sides the Indus culture bracketed above and below by other cultures, and would amply reward a single season's excavation carried out with skill and purpose.

Lacking conclusive evidence from a number of sites, we can assume from what has already been found at Dabar Kot, at various sites in Sind, and at Kot Diji, twenty-five miles east of Mohenjo-daro, that beginning about 3000 B.C. the farmer-hunters of the hill communities in Baluchistan began to move down into the Indus Valley. At Kot Diji, where there are sixteen successive levels of occupation, the third from the bottom has been given a carbon-14 dating of 2700 B.C. The three topmost layers were identified by characteristic Indus pottery and other artifacts. The fourth layer revealed both Indus and pre-Indus material; the layer below that, which has been dated to about 2400 B.C., showed evidence of a conflagration and contained objects so different from those found in the topmost layers as to make it certain that they belonged to an antecedent culture, which has now been labelled Kot Dijian. All the layers below this belonged to the same pre-Indus culture. Because of the resemblances between Kot Dijian artifacts and those found in the Baluchistan region, it now seems likely that these early valley dwellers were directly related to the tribal immigrants who had begun moving down from the northern hills in the early third millennium. But these early settlers lacked the distinguishing characteristics – and techniques – of the civilization builders who followed them several centuries later.

The implication is fairly clear; newcomers arrived in the middle of the third millennium B.C. Probably they took and then burned the settlement, and afterwards rebuilt it, living there and establishing their own culture. They were more advanced than the people they superseded. For example, copper and bronze occurred in the Indus layers, together with walls of baked brick. The lower levels contained only stone tools and stone and mud-brick foundations. Similarly, at Harappa, excavations in 1946 revealed in the occupation layers below the citadel defences a non-Indus culture related to those of north Baluchistan; and a similar situation was found to exist at Amri, south of Mohenjo-daro in Sind. Other sites await the spade, and no doubt a time will come when we shall be able to trace the newcomers back to their homelands, just as

Pot, found in Baluchistan, but Iranian in shape.

in Mesopotamia we can trace back the highly civilized Sumerians to the al 'Ubaid and Tell Halaf peoples.

The most important thing these mountain people who were to build the Indus culture brought with them to the valley was not, perhaps, their bronze tools or weapons, but the concept of a civilized society. Such a society, whose people had the knowledge of writing and led a complex, organized life centred in cities, had earlier developed in Mesopotamia. It may well have been that the hill people of Baluchistan were aware of these developments beyond the Iranian plateau in Mesopotamia and profited from this knowledge.

For centuries they had lived a closed, precarious, and difficult existence in their mountain homes, managing only to grow enough food and raise sufficient stock to eke out what they gained by hunting. But not far away lay the broad, fertile plains of the Indus and its tributaries, a dangerous land of deep jungle and wild animals. Like the valleys of the Tigris and Euphrates it could, if tamed and civilized, yield a richer and more abundant life. The land, perpetually fertilized by river-borne mud, was rich. There was an abundance of game and fish. And the river itself provided a natural highway linking and uniting a vast area. At some time, perhaps cautiously at first, the people from the hills began to move down on to the plain. The diseases that only recently began to yield to modern science surely took a heavy toll. There were wild animals against which the only weapons were the bow and the spear, and the later settlers had to contend with hostile peoples as well. The mighty river when in flood was like a god in anger, fierce and uncontrollable, sweeping away farms, fields, men, and beasts. Yet the immigrants stayed on and fought. Thousands died, but others arrived to take their places and gradually learned to control their environment sufficiently to make urban life possible.

Within not more than a thousand years these people had created their own civilization with a heavy dependence on irrigation, flood control, and communal farming on a large scale. They built at least two big planned cities; they traded extensively with many other cultures, perhaps both by overland caravans and by small, sea-going vessels. They created a massive, if somewhat dull architecture and developed a system of pictographs, which were engraved on seals presumably used for labelling and identifying the ownership of property. And yet before the end of those ten centuries their civilization had begun to decline, and in 1500 B.C. it was overwhelmed – at least in its Indus Valley homeland – and eventually disappeared almost without trace.

Compare this relatively rapid growth and decay with the long-lived civilizations of ancient Egypt and Mesopotamia, each of which lasted three thousand years, and it will be seen that the Indus Valley culture was not the product of slow, inevitable growth. It could hardly have happened save by a conscious effort of will on the part of people who had a defined objective. This, at least, is Wheeler's theory. He writes:

> The benefits offered on so formidable a scale by an environment at the same time so vast, so exuberant, and so menacing are dependent, and dependent from the outset, upon the power of man to master and constrain. The situation was one which can have brooked no pusillanimity, no piecemeal compromise. A society strong in heart, disciplined, numerous, and imaginatively led grasped the problem and, we may be sure, simultaneously solved it; else it had perished.

In sum, we have a picture of people driven to tame and civilize a hostile but potentially rich region, perhaps inspired by the example of another group of human beings who had done the same. As an analogy, modern European civilization has roots that penetrate thousands of years into the past. The peoples of Africa, for example, will not need thousands of years to reach a similar level of civilization. So it may have been with the Indus Valley people.

Yet we have only the vaguest clues to the type of society that they created. We know practically nothing of their religion, though the presence of numerous female figurines – possibly of a fertility goddess – suggests that in the Indus Valley, as in Sumer and Crete, the earliest deities were female. And since in Egypt, Sumer, Hatti, and other centres of civilization the intellectual leaders were the priests who claimed to understand and control the forces of nature, it is reasonable to assume that a similar situation would have applied in the Indus

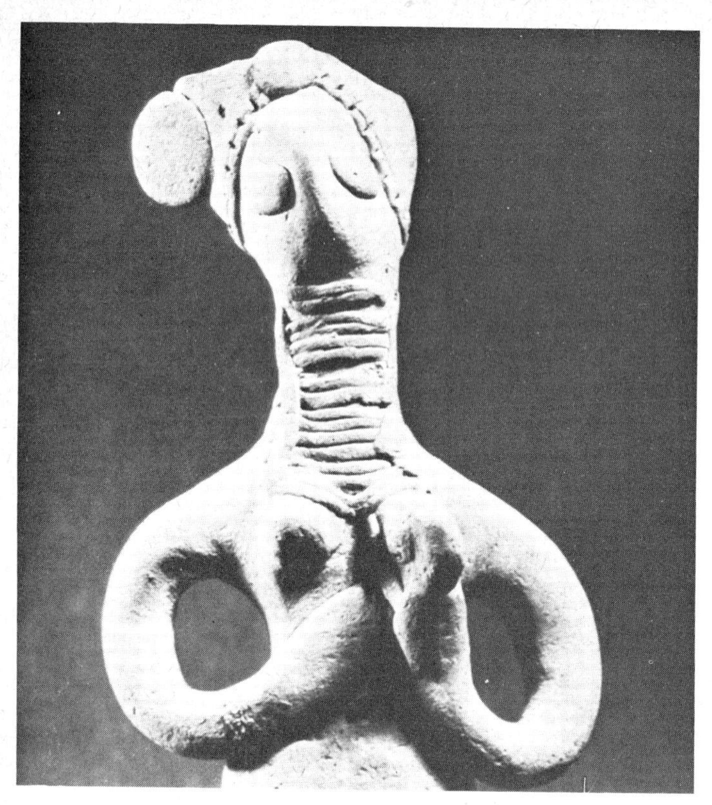

Clay figurine.

Valley. Yet to date, no temples have been positively identified, though on seals and among the statues of stone, terracotta, and bronze unearthed at Harappa and Mohenjo-daro are figures that may represent gods. One seal depicts a three-faced figure sitting on a low stool flanked by a buffalo and a rhinoceros; below the stool are two antelopes or goats. Sir John Marshall has suggested that this figure may have been the prototype of the later Hindu god Ṣiva, in his aspect as lord of beasts.

There are also small clay statuettes representing female figures, nude except for intricate necklaces and large, wide-spreading head-dresses. Some of the figures have a cup on each side of the head-dress, and from the smoke stains occasionally

Steatite seal depicting three-faced god.

found in them it has been assumed that they were used for burning incense. Occasionally one finds seals with figures reminiscent of certain Sumerian mythological scenes; for example, a horned tiger being attacked by a bull-man or minotaur recalls numerous Sumerian representations of battles between minotaurs and various composite animals.

Besides the seals with Sumerian motifs, there is evidence of another Mesopotamian parallel with the Indus Valley culture; this is the basic concept of controlling a flooding river by diverting its waters, in order to irrigate and fertilize large tracts of arid land. Yet in most respects the Harappan civilization was quite individual. The plans of the Indus cities, with their citadels and granaries, the construction of the buildings, the pottery, tools, and weapons, the statuary and ornaments bear little resemblance to their counterparts in Sumer and other cultures. Those Sumerian objects that have been found were clearly imported in the normal processes of trade. The entrepôt of this trade, Telmun, can probably be identified with the island Bahrein in the Persian Gulf, reached by sailing down the Indus and then westward along the coast of the Arabian Sea. Sumerian cuneiform tablets describe Telmun as a trading centre and refer occasionally to a land called Meluhha, which may have been the Indus Valley.

The inhabitants of the Indus were a great trading people. They imported not only Sumerian products but gold from southern India, silver, copper, and lapis lazuli from Afghanistan, and turquoise from Iran; in return their merchants may have shipped abroad copper, stone, ivory, wood and certain animals. Among their agricultural products were wheat, barley, melons, peas, sesame, and possibly dates, and they domesticated humped cattle, buffaloes, and possibly horses, asses, cats, pigs, and camels· They also grew cotton and exported it to Sumer; they are the earliest people known to have cultivated this plant.

The Harappans had an effective system of weights and measures, a necessity for both the domestic and the foreign commerce of their thriving cities. At the Indus sites weights have been found ranging from very large to tiny units. The former are in some cases so large that ropes and metal rings were required to hoist them; the smallest weights were probably used by jewellers. The higher weights, along with measures of length, followed the decimal system, although the binary system was used for lower denominations.

But the principal source of wealth in the Indus Valley was the land, which, though richly fertile, had to be protected. Bitter experience must have taught the people how violent and unpredictable were the Indus floods. They learned to build dikes and dams and to raise their cities on mounds out of reach of the floodwaters. It must have been a constant, bitter struggle involving the communal effort of many thousands. Admittedly the Indus settlers had one notable advantage over the Egyptians and the Sumerians, who had to learn the technique through trial and error over a vast period of time. As Wheeler says, the Indus people at least had the assurance that it had been done before and could therefore be done again. Even so, the Indus presented its own special problems, which the settlers solved, or partially solved, in their own individual way. The state granaries, huge and severely functional, drew their supplies from a wide area, as has already been pointed out. At Mohenjo-daro archaeologists were able to identify an unloading area into which grain wagons were evidently driven. Above this area was a platform on to which the sheaves of barley could be hauled by ropes, after which they would be stacked in the huge castle-like structure, whose steep, forbidding walls were clearly designed to resist attack. For grain was life, and the dusty, sweating drivers with their ox-carts, bringing in the harvest from fields far out across the plain, knew that by so doing they were protecting themselves against the results of flood, famine, and foreign invasion.

However, it is only fair to mention that this theory is not universally shared by archaeologists. Some students of the Indus Valley civilization have put forward a different interpretation, according to which the great cities of Harappa and Mohenjo-daro were merely cult centres dedicated to the worship of a god or several gods; the tributes of grain were intended for the deity; and the real centres of the Indus Valley civilization were the smaller towns and villages. It is a theory that has few adherents, for the ancient civilizations of which we have better records – Egypt, Sumer, and Crete – were orientated on palaces or cities in which lived not only the temporal or spiritual rulers of the state, but the administrators, record keepers, and tax collectors who controlled its economy. Nevertheless, it is true that to date nothing resembling the files of accounts, receipts, and tax returns – such as one might expect to find at an archaeological city-site – has turned up at either Harappa or Mohenjo-daro.

What sort of life was lived by the inhabitants of Harappa and Mohenjo-daro during the millennium that their civilization endured? Again we have to rely on remains of buildings, tools, weapons, pottery, and a few examples of statuary, seals, and ornaments. Yet much may be learned even from this sparse evidence. The cities were planned with an eye to convenience, efficiency, cleanliness, and protection from the baking sun. The sanitary system and the numerous baths would have helped to keep down the plagues and epidemics that threaten large communities of people, especially in hot countries. Some of the buildings were commodious and exhibit a certain bourgeois comfort, if not grace, and even the smallest dwellings, though cramped and of dreary uniformity, were probably no worse than the homes of millions of Indian and Pakistani artisans today. In the important respects of sanitation and water supply, they were superior.

Rich burials, like those that tell us so much about the peoples of Egypt and Sumer, have not yet been encountered; such graves as have been discovered are evidently those of average citizens. Several pots and trinkets accompany a corpse, and that is all. Nor is there anything strikingly beautiful in the pottery, though it is interesting that some pottery fragments have been found inscribed with those intriguing pictographs that have so far defied interpretation. (Michael Ventris, decipherer of the Cretan Linear B script was about to begin work on the Indus pictographs when he died.) Such jewellery as has been found, especially the necklaces of gold, faience, carnelian, and steatite, is pleasing but unremarkable. Perhaps the most beautiful, as well as the most characteristic, Indus artifacts are the tiny seals, about an inch in width. Unlike the cylindrical Sumerian seals, these are usually square, though some are disk-shaped and a few cylindrical examples have been found. Each was carved in stone with a minute but delicately executed design, usually featuring an animal, and from these we know the types of wild beasts with which the Indus Valley folk were familiar. They include the crocodile, rhinoceros, elephant, tiger, and antelope; also a strange ox-like creature that appears to have only one horn. (Sir Mortimer Wheeler has noted that according to both Aristotle and Ctesias, a Greek historian, the unicorn came from India.)

The seals were usually perforated for hanging around the neck or wrist and usually had short pictographic inscriptions. These may have been names, though not necessarily always of

Steatite seals.

individuals; some may indicate a title or a trade. The seals were probably used for stamping the clay sealings that identified the ownership of certain goods – jars of oil or wine, for instance, bales of cloth, or other properties. A similar method was used in both Mesopotamia and Egypt. Apart from their interest as minute works of art, these seals may perhaps eventually provide clues that will lead archaeologists to the original homelands of the Indus Valley people; they are so characteristic of this culture that they provide a readily recognizable clue to an Indus site, wherever it may be found. In contrast to the currently favoured theory that the origins of the Indus people may ultimately be discovered in both Iran and Baluchistan, Stuart Piggott, an authority on Indus Valley archaeology, has pointed out that virtually no seals have been found in the Baluchistan settlements; he maintains that the people who carried what was to become Harappan culture down from the uplands must therefore have come directly from Iran, and not from Baluchistan.

Few examples of Indus statuary, either in stone or bronze; have been found; those that exist indicate that Harappan

Tiger portrayed on a seal.

artisans were not particularly interested in portraying the human form. An exception is the slim, nubile figure of a dancing girl, her hand provocatively resting on her hip, and naked save for her numerous armlets. This little bronze figurine has such a contemporary Indian quality as to make it probable that artistic elements of the Indus Valley culture, as well as the religious customs already mentioned, were absorbed by the Aryan invaders and transmitted to later Indian cultures. Of the small stone sculptures, perhaps the most striking is the steatite figure of a bearded man, found at Mohenjo-daro. It has a powerful but sinister face, with narrow eyes, prognathous jaw, and receding forehead, impressive in a somewhat repellent way – the kind of face one can well imagine frowning down from the citadel on the ranks of labourers pounding grain on the work platforms.

There is a large number of little terracotta models of animals, executed with keen observation of the character of the beast depicted, and with masterly technique. There are also terracotta toy carts with movable wheels, much like the peasant carts seen in India today; small, clay, box-like shapes, thought

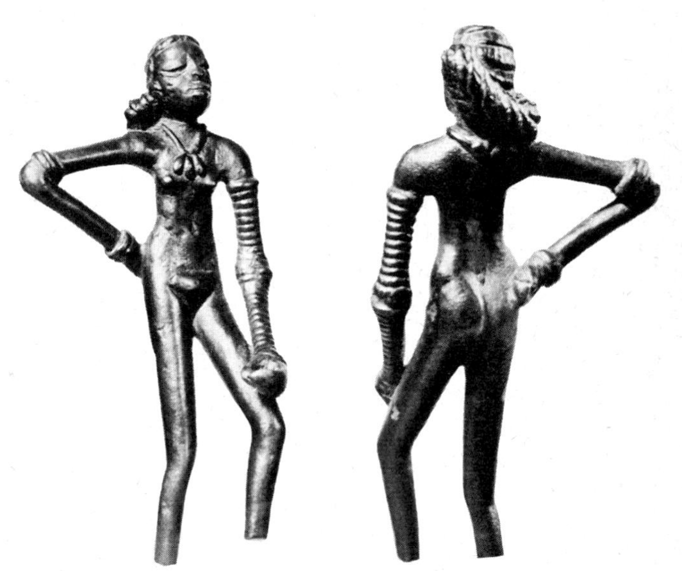

Bronze figure of a dancing-girl, 4½ inches in height.

230 Stone sculpture from the Indus Valley.

Terracotta bull.

Monkey, finished with faience glaze.

Terracotta toy carts.

to have been mousetraps, and terracotta rattles and dice have also been found. The dice remarkably resemble those used in games today, but the dotted markings on opposite sides do not add up to seven; one dot appears opposite two, instead of opposite six.

Finally we must ask why the Indus Valley civilization, after only one thousand years of existence, failed and disappeared. The most widely accepted answer, previously discussed in connexion with the *Rig-Veda*, is that it was overthrown about 1500 B.C. by the Aryan invaders under their war god Indra, the fort-destroyer. The Aryans seem to have come from the southern slopes of the Himalayas and may have been related to other warrior peoples who were moving into Asia Minor and Greece both at the beginning and at the end of the second millennium B.C. One may speculate that *Hari-Yupuya*, described in the *Rig-Veda* as the site of an Aryan victory, may have been Harappa. And at Mohenjo-daro the excavators came upon piles of skeletons of men, women, and children who had been cut down, stabbed, or clubbed to death and left to rot where they fell. It was a grim sight; in one house thirteen skeletons, still wearing rings and bracelets, lay sprawled in the agony of death. Sword cuts in the skulls of two skeletons showed how they had perished. Not far away was a public well, and here two other skeletons, one of them female, lay stretched across the stones, apparently struck down as they had tried to escape. In another place lay nine more contorted skeletons, five of which were those of children. All this pitiful human debris lay in the highest level of the city, the last one inhabited by Indus-culture people.

This is the catastrophic end of the story uncovered by archaeologists. As they sank their shafts through the layers of the city they revealed a record of progressive deterioration and decay. At the lower levels were fine, well-made buildings of impressive size and construction. But higher up in the mound the buildings became shoddier and smaller. As generation succeeded generation, each generation building on the partly demolished structures of its forebears, the living quarters became more cramped, the construction progressively poorer. It seemed as if 'squatters' had moved in, breeding prolifically, no doubt, and no longer enjoying the wealth that the city had been able to command in the days of its greatness. It was as if once-dignified town mansions had deteriorated until they had become slum dwellings.

Finally, it may be surmised, the state decayed to the point where its defences were neglected, and the Aryans moved down into the valley just as the ancestors of the Indus people had moved down in the distant past. Indra had come, and the thousand-year experiment in civilization was at an end.

What caused this decline? Groping in semi-darkness, without the light of written records or the testimony of neighbouring or successor peoples, we can find no certain answer, but must fall back on theory. There could have been a break-up of the strong controlling power, and a succession of impotent rulers; there could have been a switching of trade routes, or a deterioration of the soil, which if neglected soon becomes saline, as one can see in the Sind desert today. (The white crust on the surface has been described by one writer as 'a satanic mockery of snow'.) Or there could have been a breakdown in the vast system of controls needed to hold in check the floods of the great river.

One ingenious theory is based on the simple fact that in building and rebuilding their cities, towns, and villages the Indus Valley people used enormous amounts of baked bricks. Baking naturally needs fire, and the principal fuel in the Indus would have been timber. Five thousand years ago large forests grew on the hills bordering the valley. The remorseless stripping of this forest cover over a period of ten centuries could well have increased the flooding of the Indus, just as deforestation has altered the climate of other lands; the heavy rainfall, no longer partially absorbed by vegetation, could have stripped off the surface soil and swelled the already affluent river to unmanageable proportions. Against such power the highest dikes would fail unless continually rebuilt and maintained. The results of such neglect may well be imagined. (It must be remembered too that only within the last century have we begun to understand the relationship between deforestation, soil erosion, and flooding.)

Compared with the much richer and better known civilizations of Egypt and Sumer, the Indus Valley civilization surely seems a far less dramatic and splendid achievement. We cannot tell how much of its contribution has been permanently lost, or what remains to be learned – especially not until the the inscriptions are deciphered; even the incomplete picture we now have of the Harappans in their bustling cities may prove to be inaccurate. Yet we can respond to the drama that lies in the total effort of a people who after untold centuries of hard-won existence in the mountains of south-eastern Iran and Baluchistan suddenly exploded into the fertile but perilous valley of the Indus. They cleared the jungle, fought the wild beasts, tamed the flooding river, planned and built their cities, and created within a relatively short time a thriving civilization. We do not know who they were or, with any certainty, where they came from. Gods, kings, heroes, thinkers, poets, all alike are forgotten. When we first encounter them they are already in possession of a mature, highly developed culture; we know nothing of the early failures that must have occurred before they secured a foothold in that untamed land. But we do know that they succeeded, and that it was through their toil that a true civilization was born.

Guide to Further Reading

EGYPT

Aldred, C., *The Egyptians*, Thames & Hudson Ltd, 1961
Baikie, J., *Egyptian Antiquities in the Nile Valley*, Methuen, 1932
Breasted, J. H., *A History of Egypt*, Hodder & Stoughton, 1946
Breasted, J. H., *Ancient Records of Egypt*, Chicago University Press, 1906
Carter, H., *The Tomb of Tutankhamun*, London, 1924–6
Cottrell, L., *The Lost Pharaohs*, Evans, 1949
Cottrell, L., *Life Under the Pharaohs*, Evans, 1955
Cottrell, L., *Lady of the Two Lands*, Evans, 1966
Desroches-Noblecourt, C., *Tutankhamen*, *The Connoisseur* and Michael Joseph, 1963; Penguin Books, 1965
Edwards, I. E. S., *The Pyramids of Egypt*, Penguin Books, 1947
Erman, A. (trans. Blackman, A. M.), *The Literature of the Ancient Egyptians*, Methuen, 1927
Emery, W. B., *Archaic Egypt*, Penguin Books, 1961
Gardiner, Sir A. H., *Egypt of the Pharaohs*, Clarendon Press, 1961
Glanville, S. R. K. (Ed.), *The Legacy of Egypt*, Clarendon Press, 1953
Lucas, A., *Ancient Egyptian Materials and Industries*, Edward Arnold, 1962

MESOPOTAMIA

Buckingham, J. S., *Travels in Mesopotamia*, London, 1827
Budge, E. A. W., *By Nile and Tigris*, London, 1920
Cottrell, L., *The Anvil of Civilisation*, Faber & Faber, 1958
Gadd, C. J., *The Stones of Assyria*, Chatto & Windus, 1936
Koldewey, R., *The Excavations at Babylon*, London, 1914

Kramer, S., *History Begins at Sumer*, Thames & Hudson, 1958
Layard, A. H., *Discoveries in the Ruins of Nineveh and Babylon*, London, 1853
Lloyd, S., *Foundations in the Dust*, Penguin Books, 1955
Woolley, Sir L., *Ur Excavations* (3 vols.), Kegan Paul, 1934–9
Woolley, Sir L., *Ur of the Chaldees*, Penguin Books, 1938

THE INDUS VALLEY CIVILIZATION

Mackay, Ernest, *The Indus Civilisation*, Lovat Dickson & Thompson, 1953
Marshall, Sir J. H., *Revealing India's Past*, India Society, 1959
Wheeler, Sir Mortimer, *The Indus Civilization*, Cambridge University Press, 1953
Wheeler, Sir Mortimer, *Early India and Pakistan*, Thames & Hudson, 1959

Acknowledgements

Grateful acknowledgement is made for permission to quote from the following works:
J. H. Breasted, *Development of Religion and Thought in Ancient Egypt*, Charles Scribner's Sons, New York. D. G. Bridson, *The Quest of Gilgamesh*, British Broadcasting Corporation, London. C. W. Ceram, *The Secret of the Hittites*, Alfred A. Knopf Inc., N. Y. Albert Champdor, *Babylon*, G. P. Putnam's Sons, N. Y. Edward Chiera, *They Wrote on Clay*, University of Chicago Press, copyright 1938 the University of Chicago. Adolf Erman, *The Literature of the Ancient Egyptians*, Methuen & Co. Ltd, London (spelling of names revised by permission of the publisher). Joan Evans, *Time and Chance*, Longmans, Green & Co. Ltd, London. Henri Frankfort, *Ancient Egyptian Religion*, Columbia University Press, N. Y.; *Kingship and the Gods*, University of Chicago Press, copyright 1948 the University of Chicago. Sir Alan Gardiner, *Egypt of the Pharaohs*, The Clarendon Press, Oxford. E. O. James, *The Ancient Gods*, G. P. Putnam's Sons. Robert Koldewey, *Excavations at Babylon*, trans. Agnes S. Johns, Macmillan & Co., London. Samuel Noah Kramer, *History Begins at Sumer*, The Falcon's Wing Press, Indian Hills, Colorado. Miriam Lichtheim, 'The Songs of Harpers', *Journal of Near Eastern Studies*, vol. IV, no. 3, 1945, The University of Chicago. Daniel David Luckenbill, *Ancient Records of Assyria and Babylonia*, by permission of the University of Chicago Press, copyright 1926 the University of Chicago. Henry Frederick Lutz, *Selected Sumerian and Babylonian Texts*, The University Museum, University of Pennsylvania, Philadelphia. Svend Aage Pallis, *The Antiquity of Iraq*, Ejnar Munksgaard A/S, Copenhagen. James B. Pritchard, ed., *Ancient Near Eastern Texts Relating to the Old Testament*, copyright 1955 Princeton University Press, Princeton. Sir Osbert Sitwell, *Escape With Me*, Macmillan

& Co., London (by permission of David Higham Associates Ltd). George Steindorff and Keith C. Seele, *When Egypt Ruled the East*, University of Chicago Press, copyright 1942 and 1957 the University of Chicago. Dirk J. Struik, *A Concise History of Mathematics*, copyright 1948 Dover Publications Inc., published by Dover Publications Inc., New York 14, N. Y., passage reprinted through permission of the publisher. Sir Mortimer Wheeler, *Early India and Pakistan*, Frederick A. Praeger Inc. H. E. Winlock, *Models of Daily Life in Ancient Egypt*, The Metropolitan Museum of Art, N. Y.

PICTURE CREDITS

The source of each picture is listed below. Its title or description appears after the page number, which is in italic type, and is followed by the original location, where possible, and the present location. Where two or more pictures appear on one page, the references are separated by dashes.

Frontispiece Hypostyle hall, Karnak. (Hirmer) *10* Sphinx from Giza. (Hassia) *17* Fishing relief, Saqqara. (Sameh) *20* Knife. Louvre (Giraudon) *23* Narmer palette, one side. Cairo (Hassia) *24* Narmer palette, detail. Cairo (Foto Marburg) *28–9* Delinquent tax-payers relief, Saqqara. (Oriental Institute, University of Chicago) *30* Step pyramid, Saqqara. (Hirmer) *31* Pyramids of Giza. (George Holton, Photoresearchers) *32* Cheops. Cairo (Walter Sanders, courtesy *Life* Magazine) *34–5* Papyrus. Cairo (Hassia) *37* Painting from tomb of Horemheb, Saqqara. (Duncan Edwards, Freelance Photographers Guild) *38* Djoser relief, Saqqara. (Hirmer) *44–5* Force-feeding fowl relief. Berlin (Grantz-Giraudon) *46* Mycerinus and queen. (Museum of Fine Arts, Boston) *47* Papyrus of lady applying lip rouge. (Museo Egizio, Turin) – Lady with lotus in hair. (Staatliche Museen, Berlin) – Mirror. (Museum of Fine Arts, Boston) *48* Statuette of lady making beer. Cairo (Sameh) *49* Relief of dancers, Saqqara. (Sameh) *50* Carpenters relief, Saqqara. (Sameh) *52* Seneb and lady. Cairo (Foto Marburg) *58* Pepi I. Cairo (Hirmer) *62–3* Drawing of Egyptian ship. (*L'Illustration, Histoire de la Marine*, Paris, 1942) *64* Chephren. Cairo (James Whitmore, courtesy *Life* Magazine) *66* Sesostris III. (Metropolitan Museum of Art, Carnarvon Collection, gift of Edward S. Harkness, 1926) *71* Yacht of Meketre, detail. (Metropolitan Museum of Art, Edward S. Harkness and the Rogers Funds, 1920) *72–3* Yacht of Meketre. (Metropolitan Museum of Art, Edward S. Harkness and the Rogers Funds, 1920) *74–5* Model of Meketre inspecting cattle. Cairo (Hassia) *77* Pectoral. (Metropolitan Museum of Art, Henry Walters and the Rogers Fund, 1916) *80* Blue faience tile. (Metropolitan Museum of Art, gift of J. Pierpont Morgan, 1917) *85* Paintings of Tuthmosis III before Amen. (Egyptian Museum, Cairo) *87* Amenhotep III relief. (British Museum) *88* Akhenaten. Berlin (F. L. Kenett) *89* Queen Nefretiti. (Staatliche Museen, Berlin) *90* Akhenaten and Nefretiti relief. Berlin (F. L. Kenett) *92* Painting of harvest, tomb of Nacht. (Eygptian expedition, Metropolitan Museum of Art) *97* Temple at Deir el Bahri. (Duncan Edwards, Freelance Photographers Guild) *98* Hypostyle hall, Karnak. (Hirmer) *99* Queen Teye. (Staatliche Museen, Berlin) *102* Craftsmen relief. Cairo (Hassia) *103*

Papyrus of Ani. (British Museum) *104* Ostracon of acrobat. Museum Egizio, Turin (courtesy A. Mekhitarian) *104–5* Comic papyrus of animals. (British Museum) *106* Painting of musicians, tomb of Nacht. (Egyptian expedition, Metropolitan Museum of Art) *107* Painting of banquet. (British Museum) *109* Blind harpist relief. Leiden (F. L. Kenett) *110* Gold Coffin of Tutankhamen. Cairo (Hirmer) *111* Lion decorating a couch. Cairo (Hassia) *112–13* Panel of painted coffer. Cairo (Walter Sanders, courtesy *Life* Magazine) *117* Colossi built by Amenhotep III, Thebes. (Walter Sanders, courtesy *Life* Magazine) *124–5* Dairy frieze from al' Ubaid. Baghdad (Frank Scherschel) *128* Hoffman tablet. Collection of the General Theological Seminary, New York (Metropolitan Museum of Arts) *129* Sumerian King list. (Photograph Ashmolean Museum, Oxford) *133* Figure from Nippur. (Courtesy Joint Nippur Expedition, Oriental Institute, University of Chicago) *134–5* Figurines from Tell Asmar. Baghdad (Oriental Insitute, University of Chicago) *140* Rein ring from Ur. British Museum (Frank Scherschel) – Head-dress from Ur. (British Museum) *141* Goat and tree from Ur. (British Museum) *142* Helmet from Ur. Baghdad (Courtesy Thames & Hudson) *143* Peace standard and war standard from Ur. (British Museum) *144* Bull's head from Ur. (University Museum, University of Pennsylvania) *146* Head from Uruk. Baghdad (courtesy Helen Keiser) *147* Neo-Babylonian cylinder seal. Pierpont Morgan Library (Lee Boltin) *148* Detail from Stele of the Vultures, Lagash. Louvre (Tel-Vigneau) *150* Head of Sargon (?) from Nineveh. Baghdad (Schneider-Lengyel, courtesy Gallimard) *152* Stele of Naram-sin from Susa. Louvre (Joubert) *153* Terracotta head of divinity from Lagash. Louvre (Tel-Vigneau) *155* Gudea, governor of Lagash (Metropolitan Museum of Art, Dick Fund, 1959) *156* Aerial view of palace, Mari. (Aviation Française du Levant) *157* School benches from Mari. (Mission Archéologique de Mari) *158* Bronze lion from Temple of Dagan, Mari. (Louvre) *159* Investiture of the king of Mari. Louvre *160* Stele of Hammurabi from Susa, detail. Louvre (Giraudon) *163* Statuette from Larsa. (Louvre) *164–5* Lady with spindle from Susa. Louvre (Archives Photographiques) *166* Female. (Louvre) – Man with monkeys. (Louvre) – Votive plaque of couple. (Metropolitan Museum of Art, Rogers Fund, 1932) – Craftsman. (Louvre) – Men picking fruit, fragment. (Yale Babylon Collection) – Man riding bull. (Oriental Institute, University of Chicago) – Armed men. Louvre (Archives Photographiques) *170* Inlaid soundbox of harp from Ur, detail. (University Museum, University of Pennsylvania) *171* Assyrian relief of hero and cub from Khorsabad, detail. Louvre (Tel-Vigneau) *178–9* Plaque of Sit-Shamsi, Susa. Louvre (Giraudon) *181* Vase from Uruk. Baghdad (Frank Scherschel, courtesy *Life* Magazine) *184* Destruction of Hamanu relief. (British Museum) *187* Black obelisk from Nimrud. (British Museum) *188* Captives relief. Louvre (Tel-Vigneau) *194* Assurbanipal feasting relief from Nineveh. (British Museum) *195* Assurbanipal in chariot relief. Louvre (Giraudon) *196* Assurbanipal shooting relief. British Museum (Werner Forman) *196–7* Lion-hunt reliefs. (British Museum) *198* Campaign of Shalmaneser III bronze relief. (British Museum) *199* Winged bull from Khorsabad. Louvre (Tel-

Vigneau) *200* Cow and calf. Baghdad (courtesy M. E. L. Mallowan) *207* West gate of Babylon. (Mella-Viollet) *213* Platform, Harappa. (Patellani-Pix) *215* Mohenjo-daro. (Frances Mortimer-Rapho Guillumette) *217* Seal impression from Mohenjo-daro. National Museum of India, New Delhi (Frances Mortimer-Rapho Guillumette) *219* Pot from Baluchistan. American Museum of Natural History (Lee Boltin) *222* Female figurine from Mohenjo-daro. National Museum of Pakistan (Frances Mortimer-Rapho Guillumette) *223* Seal impression of deity from Mohenjo-daro. National Museum of India (Frances Mortimer-Rapho Guillumette) *227* Seal impressions of elephant and bull from Mohenjo-daro. National Museum of India (Frances Mortimer-Rapho Guillumette) *228* Seal impression of tiger from Mohenjo-daro. National Museum of India (Frances Mortimer-Rapho Guillumette) *229* Dancer from Mohenjo-daro, two views. National Museum of India (Frances Mortimer-Rapho Guillumette) *230* Stone bust from Mohenjo-daro. National Museum of Karachi, Pakistan (J. Powell) *231* Bull from Mohenjo-daro. National Museum of India (Frances Mortimer-Rapho Guillumette) – Monkey from Mohenjo-daro. National Museum of Pakistan (Frances Mortimer-Rapho Guillumette) *232* Cart from Chanhu-daro. (Museum of Fine Arts, Boston)

Index

NOTE. *Page numbers in italics refer to illustrations or their captions.*

More about Penguins

If you have enjoyed reading this book you may wish to know that *Penguin Book News* appears every month. It is an attractively illustrated magazine containing a complete list of books published by Penguins and still in print, together with details of the month's new books. A specimen copy will be sent free on request.

Penguin Book News is obtainable from most bookshops; but you may prefer to become a regular subscriber at 3s. for twelve issues. Just write to Dept EP, Penguin Books Ltd, Harmondsworth, Middlesex, enclosing a cheque or postal order, and you will be put on the mailing list.

Two other books of related interest published by Penguins are described on the following pages.

Note: *Penguin Book News* is not available in the U.S.A., Canada or Australia.

The Ancient Explorers

M. Cary and E. H. Warmington

Two eminent scholars – both professors in the University of London – collaborated in the writing of this volume, which remains a standard work on ancient travel and discovery. Concerned with the actual journeys made rather than with the geographical speculations of ancient scholars, they tell how, before Arabic expansion closed the gates of the Mediterranean Sea, men had coasted Western Europe and penetrated the continent south of the Danube and Rhine, sailed from Suez to Canton and probed deeply into Asia, and – even if they failed to circumnavigate Africa – had been as far as Sierra Leone and Port Delgado. They describe, too, the objects of these journeys, the crude equipment of sailors, and the scanty geographical knowledge on which they proceeded.

In this 'Hakluyt' of the ancient world one reads – often with surprise – of Greeks in India and Romans in China, of the account of the source of the Nile given by one Diogenes, and of Pytheas's extended visit to the boorish inhabitants of Britain. And it is clear that the Great Age of Discovery, in the fifteenth and sixteenth centuries, was heavily indebted to these more ancient explorers.

The Penguin Book of Lost Worlds VOLUME 2

Leonard Cottrell

This volume continues the fascinating story of those long forgotten worlds of the past which are now reconstructed for us by the magic touch of Leonard Cottrell. Volume 2 takes up the story of Crete and Mycenae, the sources of heroic legends, and unfolds their primitive Greek civilizations. It shows us the isolated world of the Hittites in Anatolia; and the story of the ancient Etruscans who threatened early Rome.

Not for sale in the U.S.A. or Canada